S0-BHV-008

PR
2983
.L382
1975

Leech, Clifford.
    Shakespeare's tragedies
and other studies in
seventeenth century drama.

PR
2983
.L382
1975

Leech, Clifford. 89018786
    Shakespeare's tragedies
and other studies in
seventeenth century drama.

GALVESTON COLLEGE
David Glenn Hunt
Memorial Library
Galveston, Texas

DAVID GLENN HUNT
MEMORIAL LIBRARY
GALVESTON COLLEGE

SHAKESPEARE'S TRAGEDIES

DAVID GLENN HUNT
MEMORIAL LIBRARY
GALVESTON COLLEGE

THE ... ...
... LIBRARY
... ...

SHAKESPEARE'S TRAGEDIES

AND OTHER STUDIES IN
SEVENTEENTH CENTURY DRAMA

by

Clifford Leech

*Lecturer in English in the
University of Durham*

GREENWOOD PRESS, PUBLISHERS
WESTPORT, CONNECTICUT

DAVID GLENN HUNT
MEMORIAL LIBRARY
GALVESTON COLLEGE

Library of Congress Cataloging in Publication Data

Leech, Clifford.
   Shakespeare's tragedies.

   Reprint of the ed. published by Chatto and Windus,
London.
    1. Shakespeare, William, 1564-1616--Tragedies.
2. English drama--17th century--History and criticism.
I. Title.
PR2983.L382 1975   822.3'3   75-16846
ISBN 0-8371-8266-2

© Clifford Leech 1950

Originally published in 1950 by Chatto and Windus,
London

Reprinted with the permission of Chatto and Windus Ltd.

Reprinted in 1975 by Greenwood Press ·
A division of Congressional Information Service, Inc.
88 Post Road West, Westport, Connecticut 06881

Library of Congress catalog card number 75-16846
ISBN 0-8371-8266-2

Printed in the United States of America

10 9 8 7 6 5 4 3 2

Acknowledgments

I wish to thank the Editors of *The Modern Language Review*, *The Durham University Journal* and *English* for permission to include certain parts of this book. Chapter I originally appeared, in an abridged form, in *English*; Chapter VIII in *The Modern Language Review*; Chapters IX and X in *The Durham University Journal*. They are here reprinted with a few minor changes.

For their kind permission to quote from copyright material I am indebted to Mr. Louis MacNeice and Messrs. Faber and Faber Ltd., to Dr. I. A. Richards and Messrs. Routledge and Kegan Paul Ltd., to Professor J. B. Trend and Messrs. W. Heffer and Sons Ltd., and to Mr. J. G. Underhill and Messrs. Charles Scribner's Sons Ltd.

C. L.

CONTENTS

PART I

Chapter I

THE IMPLICATIONS OF TRAGEDY

THE gulf between the learned use and the popular use of the same word is nowhere better illustrated than in 'tragedy'. The term is used from day to day in referring to incidents of a distressful nature, and, in so far as it is popularly used as the name of a literary type, it is applied to any play or story with an unhappy ending. This is unfortunate, for the widespread vague use of the term makes it more difficult for students to clarify their ideas on the significance of *King Lear* and the *Agamemnon*: if our labels are smudged, we are forced to make a continual effort to remind ourselves of the contents of each package. Yet here we cannot blame the journalist for the blurring of the word's meaning, for the vague use of 'tragedy' goes back to medieval times. Moreover, even those who have aimed at using the word precisely have not reached agreement concerning the nature of the literary type to which the word is, by them, applied.

The most famous definition of tragedy in medieval times is given by Chaucer in the Prologue to *The Monk's Tale*:

> Tragedie is to seyn a certeyn storie,
> As olde bokes maken us memorie,
> Of him that stood in greet prosperitie
> And is y-fallen out of heigh degree
> Into miserie, and endeth wrecchedly.

He adds that tragedies are commonly written in hexameters, but that 'many oon' has been written in prose as well as in other metres. Similarly in his translation of Boethius he adds the gloss:

> Tragedie is to seyn, a ditee of a prosperitie for a tyme, that endeth in wrecchednesse.

It is evident that, in Chaucer's view, a tragedy need not be written in dramatic form. This arose out of the break in continuity between the drama of antiquity and the drama of the medieval church, and indeed most medieval references to tragedy similarly make no mention of dramatic representation. But this is not the only omission which strikes us in Chaucer's definition, for he indicates no cause for the fall from high degree. This, however, he had to consider when writing the 'tragedies' of *The Monk's Tale*: he could not pen tales of woe without implying why the woe came about. In the opening lines of *The Monk's Tale* he averred that it was Fortune who was responsible for the change in a man's estate: capriciously she might turn her back, and man should steel himself for these methodless reversals. On the other hand, in some of the Monk's 'tragedies' a totally different idea is put forward: man is there frequently robbed of his prosperity on account of sin: Adam, for example, is turned out of Paradise 'for misgovernaunce'. Chaucer, in fact, hesitates in his conception of tragedy in much the same way as do most people who tell sad tales: at times they believe that misfortunes come because they are merited, at times they feel that there is such a thing as bad luck: they waver between a planned universe of rewards and punishments and a chaotic universe in which chance operates without motive.

Yet if Chaucer's use of the term is the common one, we should recognise that literary theorists have been justified in trying to use the term more precisely. They have felt that certain pieces of dramatic literature are of a special kind, leaving an impression on our minds which is peculiar to themselves, and thus demanding a special label. Aristotle in Chapter VI of *The Poetics* produced a definition of tragedy which has served as a starting-point for every modern critic who has attempted to describe the effect of plays of this kind; and though the definition is obscure in the crucial point, that of *catharsis*, it provides clear evidence that Aristotle recognised tragic plays as constituting a special *genre*. At the same time Aristotle illustrates how difficult it is to be precise concerning the nature of his *genre*: in Chapter XIII he claims that the tragic hero, 'a man not pre-eminently virtuous and just', should fall from prosperity to misery through a fatal flaw in his character or an error of judgment, and thus he defends the unhappy ending in tragedy; in Chapter XIV, however, he gives especial praise to that type of tragedy in which disaster is avoided at the last moment through the revelation of something previously unknown. The contradiction may well be due to the conflicting claims of philosophic theory and dramatic effectiveness. In any event, it may serve as a warning of the difficulty of achieving consistency in a theory of tragedy, and of deciding exactly which plays are to be accepted as tragic.

It is not my purpose here to consider the many explanations of *catharsis* that have been put forward from the time of the Italian Renaissance critics. In all likelihood Aristotle's notion was that tragedy served as a safety-valve, a means of freeing the mind from the pity and the fear that might otherwise enter public or private life, and Mr. F. L. Lucas may be right in his belief that Aristotle claimed this cathartic effect for tragedy as a defence against the charges of Plato.[1] But that the emotions of pity and fear are concerned in the tragic effect has not

[1] *Tragedy in Relation to Aristotle's Poetics*, 1927, p. 33.

been disputed by any subsequent theorist. Dr. I. A. Richards, indeed, has seen these two emotions as opposing forces which tragedy brings into a state of equilibrium. For him the tragic effect is the achievement of a state of repose in the nervous system, a repose without inertia because it is the result of a perpetual opposition:

> Pity, the impulse to approach, and Terror, the impulse to retreat, are brought in Tragedy to a reconciliation which they find nowhere else, and with them who knows what other allied groups of equally discordant impulses. Their union in an ordered single response is the *catharsis* by which Tragedy is recognised, whether Aristotle meant anything of this kind or not. This is the explanation of that sense of release, of repose in the midst of stress, of balance and composure, given by Tragedy, for there is no other way in which such impulses, once awakened, can be set at rest without suppression.[1]

But the difficulty about this is that Dr. Richards does not tell us what it is that we feel an impulse to approach and a simultaneous impulse to retreat from. We feel pity—or perhaps sympathy would be the better word—with reference to the tragic hero and to other characters who are involved in disaster, but we are not terrified by him or them. Even where the tragic hero, like Orestes or Macbeth, causes fear to the other characters, we do not share their feelings. Our fear is aroused by the picture of the universe that the tragic writer presents, we are impelled to retreat from the contemplation of evil, we should like to shut our eyes if we could. If, therefore, the pity and the fear are aroused by different stimuli, it is difficult to see how any balancing of them can be other than fortuitous. Our sympathy with Hamlet is greater than our sympathy with Othello, because most of us find Hamlet the more attractive character: yet it would be a rash assumption that the play of *Hamlet* arouses more terror than the play of

[1] *Principles of Literary Criticism*, 1934, pp. 245–6.

Othello. ⸢Moreover, Dr. Richards's view of tragedy is weighted on the therapeutic side. He claims that it makes us feel that 'all is right . . . in the nervous system',[1] but he neglects that part of our experience which is the recognition that the dramatist's view of the universe is terrible as well as strengthening.⸥

Yet the idea that the tragic effect resides in an equilibrium of opposing forces does seem to correspond with our experience. After witnessing a successful performance of one of Shakespeare's four great tragedies, or of Webster's *The Duchess of Malfi*, or of the *Agamemnon*, our state of mind is active, and yet active to no immediate end: we are in a state of unusual stimulation, and yet we are more inclined to contemplate the experience than to plan our future conduct: we have seen a picture of evil, but it has neither palsied our faculties nor aroused us to struggle against it.

It is not surprising, therefore, that Professor Una Ellis-Fermor has also seen a balance of opposing forces in the effect of tragedy.[2] For her the balance is between the view that the world is controlled by an alien and hostile destiny and the view that somehow this apparent evil may be explained in terms of good. She points out that in the *Agamemnon* and the *Choëphoroe* Aeschylus presents the evil of things through the actions and the words of the actors, and through the speeches of the Chorus suggests that outside the human world there is a divine organisation of things. In Shakespeare, she suggests, the fact that such characters as Cordelia and Kent can exist must lead to what she calls a 'positive' interpretation—that is, an idea that the universe is under benevolent direction. Feeling, perhaps, that the indications of goodness are in some indubitable tragedies rather too slight, Professor Ellis-Fermor adds that the very principle of order apparent in

[1] *Ibid.*, p. 246.   [2] *The Frontiers of Drama*, 1945, pp. 127–47.

the formal articulation of tragic plays acts as a counter-poise to the evil chaos that seems to prevail. Her view, in brief, is that the tragic equilibrium consists in the simul-taneous holding in the mind of the two conflicting ideas: that the universe is divinely directed and that it is devil-ridden. She implies, however, that this equilibrium is impermanent, that the tragic writer may find his way beyond it to an acceptance of the idea of divine control, and she refers here to Shakespeare's final romances as evidence that Shakespeare escaped from the dark vision of *Othello* and *Lear*.

The difficulty in Professor Ellis-Fermor's position is that the indications of a divinely controlled universe are in many tragedies scarcely sufficient to counterpoise the presentation of evil. It is not enough that in *Othello* we have characters who mean no harm: Othello and Des-demona are well-intentioned enough, but their disaster comes upon them through his credulity and her lack of directness: in view of the magnitude of the suffering that is brought about by these comparatively minor faults, it is difficult to see that their good qualities point to a divinely controlled universe. And the control of art need suggest nothing more than that man has a certain faculty for ordering part of his experience: it does not transform the nature of that experience, and it does not necessarily suggest that either he or a creator can control the totality of experience.

That there is an equilibrium of forces in the tragic effect I think we can admit, but Professor Ellis-Fermor has looked too far in trying to reconcile the tragic and the Christian pictures of life. We need to examine the tragic picture in more detail—to consider, banishing pre-sup-positions as far as we can, the view of life offered to us by plays that we will all agree to have a similar effect on us, plays that we will not hesitate to call 'tragic'.

Not only are great evil and suffering presented in such plays but there is no comprehensible scheme of rewards and punishments suggested. Oedipus sins, as Aristotle puts it, through an error of judgment, yet he is led to a state of mind where even the thought of death is no escape from the horror; Othello is induced to murder his innocent wife and then to realise his mistake: only suicide offers itself as a way out; Desdemona and Ophelia are guilty of nothing more than weakness, yet they are destroyed; Lear is hot-tempered and foolish, yet no one will claim that he deserved to endure madness and the storm on the heath; Cordelia refuses to play her father's game, and is hanged for it; Gloucester begets Edmund, and his eyes are plucked out; Webster's Duchess of Malfi loves and marries her steward Antonio, and on that account is slowly tortured to death. Moreover, the plays frequently include a number of minor characters whose sudden and cruel deaths do not arise out of any fault of their own: Lady Macduff and her son, Polonius, Rosencrantz and Guildenstern, the brave servant in *King Lear* who tries to save Gloucester from blindness, the virtuous Marcello in Webster's *The White Devil*—all these can hardly be said to get their deserts. It is true that in some tragedies the final disaster springs from an evil act on the part of the hero—*Macbeth* and the plays of Marlowe come quickly to the mind—but even there we feel no satisfaction in the hero's punishment. Rather, we have a feeling that his initial conduct was hardly within his own control: Macbeth was singularly unfortunate in the joint temptation from the witches and his wife, and the witches' prophecy suggests from the beginning that his crime was predetermined; Marlowe's heroes are felt to act as they do because the world is what it is, a world which presents a perpetual challenge to the man of high courage. Thus we feel no desire to rejoice when the perpetrator of evil is brought to his doom, and at the same time we are aware that many characters in these plays are subjected to an evil for which they are in no way responsible.

Nor is there in great tragedy the suggestion that these things will be put right in another world. It is true that in comparatively minor works like Kyd's *The Spanish Tragedy* we are assured in an epilogue that the hero and his supporters will find their way to the Elysian Fields while their adversaries will know infernal tortures, but in *Othello* and *Lear* and *Macbeth* there is no such emphasis on a compensatory future life. Othello contemplates immortality only with horror:

> O ill-starr'd wench!
> Pale as thy smock! when we shall meet at compt,
> This look of thine will hurl my soul from heaven,
> And fiends will snatch at it. (V. ii.)

Cleopatra assumes a heavenly encounter with Antony, and fears that Iras will get to him first:

> This proves me base:
> If she first meet the curled Antony,
> He'll make demand of her, and spend that kiss
> Which is my heaven to have. (V. ii.)

Her speech is no consolation to the audience, who are made to feel only the strange limitations of this late tragic figure. In *Hamlet* heavenly joys are on occasion referred to: Horatio's

> Good night, sweet prince,
> And flights of angels sing thee to thy rest! (V. ii.)

and Laertes'

> I tell thee, churlish priest,
> A ministering angel shall my sister be,
> When thou liest howling. (V. i.)

are, however, pieces of embroidery on the situation of the moment rather than functional utterances in the play.

Indeed, *Hamlet* is essentially a play of doubt concerning what happens after death, and we are likely to agree that in no Shakespearian tragedy are we made to think of the characters as emerging from their suffering into the beatific vision: the stresses they encounter are not preparations for a future life but are inescapable conditions of the only world in which they certainly have an existence. What may or may not happen after death is something that the tragic dramatist normally leaves out of consideration: on the rare occasions when he does consider it, as Marlowe does in *Faustus*, it is to see it as part of the evil which his tragic hero must endure.

Because of the apparent absence of a kindly or just disposition of things in the world and because of his disregard of a future life, the tragic dramatist inevitably sees the gods as remote, if not as beings actively hostile to man. Perhaps the remoteness of the gods is given most succinct expression in Webster's *The Duchess of Malfi*, where the Duchess is subjected to intense mental torture before she is finally killed. Hearing false news of the death of her husband and children, she cries out that she could curse the stars: Bosola, her enemies' instrument, lets her tongue run on in grief for a few moments and then bids her look heavenward:

> Look you, the stars shine still.   (IV. i.)

All seventeenth-century English tragedy is, indeed, marked by a feeling that, if there are gods who control the universe, they are far away from men, and indifferent to the individual's fate. Sometimes this sense of remoteness becomes sharpened into a belief that the gods are malicious, enjoying the impotence and the suffering in the world beneath them. Gloucester's cry in his despair:

> As flies to wanton boys, are we to the gods,
> They kill us for their sport.   (IV. i.)

is almost paralleled by this piece of bitterness from *The Duchess of Malfi*:

> We are merely the stars' tennis-balls, struck and bandied
> Which way please them. (V. iv.)

But these are dramatic utterances, mere exclamations of the characters' despair, and are no more to be taken as expressing the totality of the playwright's attitude than are the words of Horatio and Laertes, already quoted, envisaging post-lethal joys. In the tragedies of the Greeks the gods intervene more directly than in Elizabethan tragedy, but there, too, there is no assurance of an even-handed justice in the fates of men, and no suggestion that man can find his compensation in an after-life. When, as in the *Eumenides*, the dramatist tries to humanise the justice of the gods, the play becomes more of a civic pageant than a tragedy: the acquittal of Orestes through the casting-vote of Pallas answers no questions but diverts the spectators' emotions into a new, and non-tragic, direction. But when a play is consistently tragic, the Greek writer does not see a man's problems as solved by a mere appeal to the Gods.

Nevertheless, it is noticeable that tragedy does not necessarily or even normally present an indictment of the divine powers. Professor Ellis-Fermor is certainly right in claiming for the choric utterances in the *Agamemnon* an expression of faith in the divine plan: here, indeed, is a passage which simultaneously brings out the remoteness of Zeus and the divine guidance of man through suffering to wisdom:

> Zeus, whoever He is, if this
> Be a name acceptable,
> By this name I will call him.
> There is no one comparable

When I reckon all of the case
Excepting Zeus, if ever I am to jettison
The barren care which clogs my heart.

Not He who formerly was great
With brawling pride and mad for broils
Will even be said to have been.
And He who was next has met
His match and is seen no more,
But Zeus is the name to cry in your triumph-song
And win the prize for wisdom.

Who setting us on the road
Made this a valid law—
   'That men must learn by suffering.'
Drop by drop in sleep upon the heart
Falls the laborious memory of pain,
Against one's will comes wisdom;
   The grace of the gods is forced on us
   Throned inviolably.[1]

Man thus has no certain knowledge even of God's name, and God is without pity in his hard discipline. So, too, it is remarkable that in *King Lear* there are repeated references to divine justice. When Albany hears that Cornwall was killed immediately after he had plucked out Gloucester's eyes, his comment is:

This shows you are above,
You justicers, that these our nether crimes
So speedily can venge! (IV. ii.)

And the deaths of Goneril and Regan bring from him these words:

This judgment of the heavens, that makes us tremble,
Touches us not with pity. (V. iii.)

---

[1] *The Agamemnon of Aeschylus,* translated by Louis MacNeice, 1936, pp. 18–19.

Most striking of all is Edgar's comment to his dying brother Edmund: he sees the misery of their father as springing from the dissolute begetting of Edmund, and pronounces that

> The gods are just, and of our pleasant vices
> Make instruments to plague us:
> The dark and vicious place where thee he got
> Cost him his eyes.   (V. iii.)

This terrible sentence seems as outrageous to our moral sense as the hanging of Cordelia or the torture of Webster's Duchess. What kind of justice, we wonder, is this, which will seize on so small a fault and inflict so terrible a punishment? The 'justice' of the gods, as seen in tragedy, is as terrible as their indifference: in fact, we shall not see tragedy aright unless we recognise that the divine justice mirrored in it is an indifferent justice, a justice which cares no whit for the individual and is not concerned with a nice balance of deserts and rewards.

This justice operates like an avalanche or an echo in an enclosed space. If an evil act is committed, no matter how trifling, it will bring consequences which are far more evil than the original act. Lear, vain and delighting in power and its display, indecently demands a public profession of love from his daughters: that leads to the events of the heath, the hanging of Cordelia, the loss of Gloucester's eyes, civil war, and Lear's own death. Thyestes seduces his brother's wife, and the long train of disasters begins for the house of Atreus. Sometimes, however, it is a neutral act which provides the starting-point: the marriage of Webster's Duchess to her steward Antonio shows only a mild disregard for 'degree', but it releases the evil forces which have been stored up in the minds of her brothers. The justice of the gods consists simply in the natural law that every act must have its consequence and that the consequence will be determined by the act and its context. If the act is in any way evil or if the situation is one with evil potentialities, then a train of evil will be the result. The tragic writer believes in causation, in the doctrine that means determine ends, and in the powerlessness of the human will to interrupt a chain of disasters.

We may therefore easily understand why the revenge-motive is so common in Greek and Elizabethan tragedy: the blood-feud is the most obvious example of the kind of situation in which wrong inevitably succeeds to wrong.

In such a world-picture as the tragic writer presents to us, it may appear difficult to see how an equilibrium of forces can exist. The impact on our minds of such inhuman justice would at first sight appear only terrible and paralysing. Yet it remains true that our experience of tragic drama is not like that. When we think of Shakespeare's tragedies, of Webster's, of Marlowe's, or of modern tragedies like Mr. Eugene O'Neill's *Mourning Becomes Electra*, or Mr. Sean O'Casey's *Juno and the Paycock*, what we recall is made up of an indifferent universe and certain characters who seem to demand our admiration. Whether the characters are comparatively blameless, like Hamlet or Webster's Duchess, or deeply guilty, like Macbeth, we feel that they have a quality of mind that somehow atones for the nature of the world in which they and we live. They have, in a greater or lesser degree, the power to endure and the power to apprehend: ultimately they are destroyed, but in all their sufferings they show an increasing readiness to endure, an ever greater awareness. As the shadows gather around them, they stand up the more resolutely, they see the human situation with clearer eyes. Webster's Duchess is at the beginning of the play merely an attractive and enterprising woman, but it is when she cries, in the midst of torment: "I am Duchess of Malfi still", that we recognise her full stature.

15

Lear develops even more remarkably from a vain, hot-tempered tyrant to a man who sees the omnipresence of social wrong and the bodily distress of the poor. So, too, our attitude to Electra and Orestes and Oedipus is inevitably one of growing admiration. Because, moreover, the dramatist has made it clear that his tragic hero is human, a man with weaknesses like our own, we feel not merely admiration but pride: we are proud of our human nature because in such characters it comes to fine flower. In a planned but terrible universe we see man justifying his existence.

Thus the equilibrium of tragedy consists in a balancing of Terror with Pride. On the one hand, we are impelled to withdraw from the spectacle, to try to forget the revelation of evil methodised; on the other, we are roused to withstand destiny, to strive to meet it with the fortitude and the clear eyes of the tragic figure. This feeling of Pride comes into full existence when the hero knows his fate and contemplates it: it is essentially distinct from the *hubris* which he may display, but which we cannot share in, before his eyes are opened.

The tragic picture of the universe postulates a limited free will. Man cannot determine the pattern of event, but he is frequently responsible either for the initiation of an evil chain or for the release of evil forces latent in a situation. Moreover, his thoughts and feelings, his attitude to the enveloping situation, are in his own control: like Orestes, he can see the horror of the matricide he must commit; like Macbeth, he can recognise his own weakness and ultimately his own insignificance in the universal scheme. Some degree of free will is, indeed, essential in tragedy, for we could hardly feel proud of an automaton.

Because of its closer approximation to the everyday appearance of things, there seems to be a greater degree of free will in Elizabethan than in Greek tragedy: it seems as if Hamlet could deflect the course of the action at almost any point if he wished, while clearly Orestes and Oedipus are bound to an established pattern. But Shakespeare and his contemporaries have gone out of their way to make us realise that the pattern is preordained for their characters too: in some plays Shakespeare uses supernatural devices to indicate the course of future events— for example in *Macbeth*, *Julius Caesar* and *Antony and Cleopatra*—and always he draws his characters in such a way that there is clearly only one line of conduct possible for them in the particular situation in which they find themselves: for them it is the doom-in-the-character rather than the doom-on-the-house. Hamlet must be killed because Hamlet in his particular situation can have no other end: his fate is as inevitable as that of a man lost in the heart of a desert.

Dr. E. M. W. Tillyard has put forward an idea of tragedy that must be considered. This has, indeed, often been suggested by writers who have tried to dilute the element of Terror in tragic plays, asserting that in tragedy, as in real life, we see how man can learn and be redeemed through suffering. Dr. Tillyard's presentation of this idea is linked up with his view of the *Oresteia* and of Shakespeare's final romances. He sees tragedy as a picture of life disturbed by the intrusion of a disruptive evil force, the apparent triumph of that force, and then the reassertion of a normality which has been strengthened through trial.[1] He points to Othello's last speech, to Lear's wider sympathy near the close of his drama, to Shakespeare's own passage through the despondency of *Timon* to the serenity of *The Tempest*. Certainly our pride in Lear grows as the play proceeds, he emerges as a great figure through the increasing darkness of the situation, but this is not to say that normality resumes her reign, all the better for the

[1] *Shakespeare's Last Plays*, 1938, pp. 16–18.

testing-time. Lear dies, defeated: that is the essential reason for our Terror; our Pride comes from his acceptance and full knowledge of the situation. The potentialities of evil and suffering are as strong as ever, the gods as ruthless, man's will as powerless. At the end of a Shakespearian tragedy, as at the end of Marlowe's *Faustus* or of *Oedipus at Colonus*, we have a quiet close: words of peace are spoken, and we are conscious that the evil situation no longer exists: the forces of evil have worked themselves out: Hamlet and all his kin are dead. There is nothing reassuring in the new situation, no promise that a new chain of evil will not quickly ensue, no lesson that men or the gods have learned. No message of hope for the future has been brought. The tragic situation, it is implied, is recurrent in human life: that is why we feel Terror; because we have seen men like ourselves yet stronger than we could expect to be, we feel also Pride.

Thus the tragic picture is incompatible with the Christian faith. It is equally incompatible with any form of religious belief that assumes the existence of a personal and kindly God. For that reason we should not be surprised at the rarity of tragedy. Chaucer's view of it as a story of a fall from prosperity to wretchedness, either at the bidding of Fortune or through divine retribution, is a mixture of unconscious paganism with Christian tradition: we cannot expect to find true tragedy anywhere in the Middle Ages, except here and there in early times when literature was not thoroughly Christianised. We can indeed recognise something of the tragic spirit in English poetry before the Conquest, from *Beowulf* to *The Battle of Maldon*. But we should not look for tragedy in the drama of seventeenth-century Spain, for always there the spirit of religion burned brightly: Calderón and Lope de Vega might show evil in their plays, but it was an evil which attended on divine forgiveness or on an acceptable retribution; they might show suffering, but with them indeed it was the suffering of purgatorial fire. Nor should we look for tragedy in the classical drama of India: the gods there are seen as close to man, as his friends and teachers, ready to test human beings but ultimately to reward virtue wherever it should show itself. We can, however, find tragedy in those European countries which were brought most fully under Renaissance influences, with a weakening of medieval faith and some return to stoicism. In the atmosphere of comparative toleration under Elizabeth and James, English tragedy was especially free to develop. In seventeenth-century France, Racine could write tragically, though the form of his plays makes them appear almost like careful exercises in imitation of the classics: there is a lack of immediacy, of direct relation to the life around him, which perhaps made both the author and his audience feel safer: there was no compulsion for them to take too seriously the tragic view of things there presented. But from the seventeenth century until comparatively recent years the tragic form has been exceedingly rare, not because of a revival of religious faith, but because in these years men have not often combined a sharp sense of evil, a faith in man, and a sense of the impersonality of divine justice. In later days it is the faith in man that has been most difficult to come by, though tragedy has made an occasional appearance in modern European and American drama, and the tragic spirit has not infrequently found non-dramatic expression in the modern novel.

But whenever tragedy has come into being, its customary and right dress has been poetry. The equilibrium of Pride and Terror is, as we have seen, an opposition of persistent forces, and consequently the tragic play is characterised by strong tension. An appearance of casualness in the play will weaken the tension, and contradict the implication of a preordained pattern of event. Moreover, in order that the spectator's mind may more fully respond to the vision of evil and of human strength in defeat, the language must be finely turned. The medium of tragedy must be poetry, or at least a kind of prose which in its formal properties is clearly distinguished from the prose of the everyday, haphazard situation—not because the beauty of the words will atone for the presentation of evil, soothing our nerves and dulling our perceptions, but because only by a co-ordination of our faculties can we reach a full realisation of any complex picture of the world. Tragedy offers us a view of things which aims at comprehensiveness, and thus in its scope resembles the great religions of east and west. Like them, therefore, it needs all the resources of language for communication with men.

Chapter 2

THE TRAGIC PICTURE

ELIZABETHAN literary criticism is no longer treated
with only a mild interest and a wondering pity. Though
the best of it was written casually, by men who turned their
greater and more sustained energies into dramatic or verse
channels, we can value the *Apology for Poetry, Discoveries,*
the Campion-Daniel controversy, the Jonsonian comments
in prologue and preface, not merely for the light thrown
by them on contemporary practice, but as repositories of
seminal ideas which may still germinate in the enquiring
mind. Sidney's 'golden world' of poetry, his suggestion of
'delight' rather than laughter as the primary goal of comic
writing, Bacon's insistence on the operation of group-consciousness in the theatre, Daniel's recognition that literary
modes have no permanence in a changing society: these
are only the best-known examples of Elizabethan dicta
which no literary theorist can safely ignore. Indeed, we
have only to glance at Gabriel Harvey's *Ciceronianus,* the
lecture which he delivered at Cambridge in 1576, in his
capacity as University Praelector in Rhetoric, to see how
the critical writings of the age both mirrored and informed
its creative activity. For Harvey, the true Ciceronian will
value the best in all writers and will aim at absorbing the
wisdom and not simply the manner of Cicero himself.
Here, in the translation of Mr. Clarence A. Forbes, is part
of Harvey's peroration:

> You, sweet youths and handsome boys, if you would be true
> and not counterfeit Ciceronians, as you are true students of the
> Ciceronian eloquence and wisdom, must come to your Cicero
> with the intention and resolve that you will never open his

book without being somehow better before you close it. This means being better not only as grammarians and rhetoricians, but also as dialecticians, ethical philosophers, political philosophers, historians, and occasionally even natural scientists, juriconsults, and cosmographers. Nor will you merely make a vain display of your Ciceronianism in school and in these cloistered shades of the University, but you will proclaim it in all your associations with men and in your daily converse, at home and abroad, in leisure and in business, among the commonalty, the courtly folk, and all men—if necessary, even to the point of fighting for it.[1]

We seem to have our finger on the Elizabethan pulse here, to discern its rapid, firm beat: because Harvey and his contemporaries loved not only the stately manner but the mind veering towards action, because their philosophy was passionately held and their passion philosophically surveyed, Elizabethan literature has its characteristic urge and amplitude.

Yet in that field of activity which, during the great decade 1600–10, set the highest seal on Elizabethan literature, the field of tragic drama, contemporary criticism is singularly inadequate. True it is that Sidney, in a remarkable passage, speaks of

> the high and excellent Tragedy, that openeth the greatest wounds, and showeth forth the ·ulcers that are covered with tissue; that maketh kings fear to be tyrants, and tyrants manifest their tyrannical humours; that, with stirring the affects of admiration and commiseration, teacheth the uncertainty of this world, and upon how weak foundations gilden roofs are builded.[2]

Here Sidney seems to recognise that the tragic writer is concerned with the uncovering of uncomfortable things,

[1] *Gabriel Harvey's Ciceronianus*, with an introduction and notes by Harold S. Wilson and an English translation by Clarence A. Forbes (University of Nebraska Studies), 1945, p. 101.

[2] *English Critical Essays (Sixteenth, Seventeenth, and Eighteenth Centuries)*, edited by Edmund D. Jones (World's Classics), 1922, pp. 31–2.

hidden evils and sorrows, mutability, and the vanity of great place; our response to tragedy, he seems to imply, is blended of 'admiration and commiseration', a feeling of exaltation and pride that men can be great and a sense of a shared wretchedness. He suggests also, however, that tragedy can be reformative in showing the villainous meeting their deserts: as he puts it earlier,

> if evil men come to the stage, they ever go out (as the tragedy writer answered to one that misliked the show of such persons) so manacled as they little animate folks to follow them.[1]

Such remarks derive from the circumstances of the time, when Sidney felt impelled to defend his craft against its traducers. Neither he nor any other critic of his age considers the effect in tragedy when honoured and loved characters suffer and cruelly die. Sidney could not know of Cordelia or the Duchess of Malfi, but the same excuse is not available for later Elizabethan and Jacobean commentators. Again and again we are told that tragedy is justified because it serves dreadful warnings on those who might otherwise fall into sin or error. Thus in the dedication to *The Revenge of Bussy d'Ambois*, published in 1613, Chapman claims the following properties as 'the soul, limbs, and limits of an authentical tragedy': 'material instruction, elegant and sententious excitation to virtue, and deflection from her contrary'. It is strange to read this as a preface to Chapman's most thoughtful play, the tragedy in which the hero Clermont knowingly does evil in the accomplishment of his revenge but finds that evil action imposed upon him by the force of circumstances: the operations of destiny are nowhere in Jacobean tragedy made more explicit, yet this play is introduced to us as if it were a dramatised sermon addressed to men of free will. In the first scene of the play itself, Clermont praises the

[1] *Ibid.*, p. 23.

drama for showing the great the emptiness of their glory and the lowly the futility of their ambition: having quoted Epictetus with approval on this point, Clermont urges that the drama is justified,

> if but for this then,
> To make the proudest out-side that most swels,
> With things without him, and aboue his worth,
> See how small cause hee has to be so blowne vp;
> And the most poore man, to be grieu'd with poorenesse,
> Both being so easily borne by expert Actors.

and he adds:

> The Stage and Actors are not so contemptfull,
> As euery innouating Puritane,
> And ignorant sweater out of zealous enuie,
> Would haue the world imagine.   (I. i.)

Thus here the function of the drama is to restrain ambition and to cultivate a quiet acceptance of lowliness. Up to a point, of course, this is sound. We may be less likely to meddle, like Iago, or to kill, like Macbeth, when we have seen the tawdriness of their prize, or to repine at our sorrows when we have seen the Earl of Gloucester enduring his. Yet tragedy, we must feel, is more than a school for Stoics: we are not merely 'improved' by it, but rather energised: we learn from it not only perhaps a greater patience but also a stronger rage against the immutable stars, a more steadfast clinging to our personal life and vision. When the Duchess of Malfi cries in Act IV of her tragedy: "I could curse the stars", and Bosola taunts her a moment later with: "Look you, the stars shine still", we are given as it were the framework of the tragic idea, the conception of a universe deaf to the individual's cries and grinding him in accordance with an incomprehensible plan; when the Duchess proclaims: "I am Duchess of

Malfi still", or Shakespeare's Antony: "I am Antony yet", they are not merely echoing the cry of Seneca's Medea: "Medea superest"—they are voicing the basic tragic response, the defiant assertion of personality. Indeed, Chapman gives us this feeling strongly in Bussy, rather less strongly in Clermont: Bussy sees the vanity of human pretensions, yet he makes the stage ring with his personal defiance.

Massinger's *The Roman Actor*, which was licensed by Sir Henry Herbert on October 11, 1626, contains a spirited defence of the stage put in the mouth of Paris, the actor of the title. He claims that

> if, to inflame
> The noble youth with an ambitious heat
> T' endure the frosts of danger, nay, of death,
> To be thought worthy the triumphal wreath
> By glorious undertakings, may deserve
> Reward or favour from the commonwealth;
> Actors may put in for as large a share
> As all the sects of the philosophers.   (I. iii.)

Like Sidney, he finds little virtue in the philosopher's 'cold precept' without the poet's living example. The actor can

> fire
> The blood, or swell the veins with emulation,
> To be both good and great;

he will show Alcides achieving his labours or Scipio triumphing over Carthage. Moreover, if villainies are displayed on the stage, the villains are shown meeting punishment:

> We show no arts of Lydian panderism,
> Corinthian poisons, Persian flatteries,
> But mulcted so in the conclusion, that
> Even those spectators that were so inclined,
> Go home changed men.

The last section of the speech urges that it is not the players' fault if some members of their audience apply to themselves a portrait that has no personal intention. The speech is admirably phrased, but the attempted justification of play-acting is almost wholly beside the point. The tragedies of the early seventeenth century could not, like the film of *Henry V*, be dedicated to those who seek national glory. They are either stories of unlawful enterprise, like *Macbeth*, *The White Devil* and *'Tis Pity She's a Whore*, or of pathological weakness, like *Hamlet*, *Othello* and *The Broken Heart*, or of irremediable suffering, like *Lear* and *The Duchess of Malfi*. Moreover, we have already seen that along with the punishment of the guilty in these plays comes the unrelieved distress of those who are not more guilty than their very humanity warrants: in a world where the simplicity of Othello brings a doom at least as terrible as that decreed for Iago's duplicity, we must think of some reason for honesty other than its value as policy.

Yet it is this alleged didactic or reformative value of the drama which is urged whenever a defence is made. In the Beaumont and Fletcher *Four Plays or Moral Representations in One*, King Emanuel of Portugal, in honour of whose wedding the plays are supposed to be acted, addresses his bride in these terms after the performance of the first play:

> What hurt's now in a Play, against which some rail
> So vehemently? thou and I, my love,
> Make excellent use methinks: I learn to be
> A lawful lover void of jealousie,
> And thou a constant wife.

The play they have just seen is a tragicomedy, with virtue indeed triumphing: if it had been *Othello*, the royal bride might perhaps have looked askance at constancy's reward.

And Shakespeare in *Hamlet* half-suggests that one of the drama's functions is to make crime less attractive:

> I have heard,
> That guilty creatures sitting at a play
> Have by the very cunning of the scene
> Been struck so to the soul that presently
> They have proclaim'd their malefactions. (II. ii.)

Of course, such utterances are casually introduced, and it would be fantastically wrong to build up an idea of Fletcher's or Shakespeare's dramatic theory from so slight and almost irrelevant a basis. Yet it is significant that, when the drama and its effect are spoken of in Elizabethan and Jacobean plays, it is always in terms like these. We can only deduce from this that the writers themselves were not clear what they were doing in writing tragedy, that the impulse that led them in this direction was never fully and consciously explored. It has long been puzzling to find Webster, in the dedication to *The White Devil*, speaking of his own masterpiece in rather slighting terms: when we link this with Chapman's assertion that tragedy aims at 'material instruction, elegant and sententious excitation to virtue, and deflection from her contrary', we become aware that the tragedies of the great decade were organic growths and not planned constructions. Indeed, the failure of certain plays that aim at the tragic effect is surely due to the dramatists' imperfect grasp of their own aims: Tourneur's *The Atheist's Tragedy* and Marston's *Antonio* plays were the works of talented men, yet they are far away from inducing an effect that we can recognise as tragic: they grope into the darkness of the human situation, and bring to our touch many dreadful shapes, yet the overt 'message' supplied is optimistic and orthodox, condemning villainy and atheism and promising peace to those who live pure and obey traditional behests.

27

A glance at W. P. Barrett's *Chart of Plays* 1584–1623 [1] brings it home that nearly all the pre-Civil War tragedies of lasting value were written in the first dozen years of the seventeenth century. There belong the four major tragedies of Shakespeare, together with *Antony, Coriolanus* and *Timon*, the *Bussy, Biron* and *Chabot* plays of Chapman, Jonson's *Sejanus* and *Catiline*, Webster's *The White Devil* and *The Duchess*, Tourneur's *The Revenger's Tragedy*. Outside that period we can find Marlowe, whose strain is so different that Mr. Eliot has judged him to be a comic dramatist *in posse*, [2] and whose plays veer between an unchecked enthusiasm which the tragic writer hardly knows and a chaos of caricature which would make impossible a tragic concern with an individual's destiny; and later on we find Middleton and Massinger and Ford—Middleton very close to the great decade and almost part of it in his *The Changeling* and *Women Beware Women*; Massinger a reliable but superficial dramatist, hardly pursuing his themes with great concernment; Ford, as individual in his way as Marlowe, the one man whose poetic boldness made genuine tragedy possible in the reign of Charles—though even his work has a nostalgic ring, a forced echo which makes him an early Beddoes as well as a late Webster. Apart from these, the later years before the closing of the theatres have many self-styled tragedies and many tragicomedies which alike derive from the Beaumont and Fletcher formula: with these we need not concern ourselves, for only at rare moments, in *Thierry and Theodoret* for example, do we find a suggestion of the tragic vision in the Beaumont and Fletcher plays.

If, then, nearly all the tragic work that matters comes

---

[1] *Chart of Plays 1584–1623*, compiled by W. P. Barrett for the Shakespeare Association, 1934.
[2] *Selected Essays*, 1934, p. 125.

from a brief space within the Elizabethan and Jacobean period, we can I think assume that there were special reasons for this early decline of tragic drama. The primary reason, it appears, was that during approximately the years 1600–10 there came a phase both in the current of Elizabethan thought and in the development of the play-house that led men to the tragic idea and facilitated its dramatic expression. But the remarkable brevity of the period within which tragedy flourished was due also to the dramatists' imperfect comprehension of their own achievement. While writing plays that explored suffering and evil and that found those things an ineluctable in-heritance, while looking into the darkness and finding no stay but in man's temporarily unconquerable mind, they could still speak of 'elegant and sententious excitation to virtue' and apologise for the absence of a Chorus or Nuntius. Their approach to tragic writing, in fact, was instinctive, flowering almost unaided in the ground they stood on.

Perhaps the clearest indication of this instinctive urge towards the tragic is to be found in the prologue to Marston's *Antonio's Revenge*, which was acted in 1599 or thereabouts and conveniently ushers in the great decade. In its many anticipations of the theme and the incidents of *Hamlet*, Marston's play has some claim on a scholar's attention, but its confusion of thought and turgidity of manner blunt its dramatic effect. Only in the prologue does Marston speak out with a crabbed eloquence, find-ing first of all an appropriateness to his play's mood in the wintry season of the year, and then inviting sympathy for his characters' woes from those who have themselves known true sorrow: the pampered ones of the world, who have known only good fortune and a light heart, will be appalled by the play's darkness, will in fact recognise no link between themselves and the imagined characters.

But this part of the prologue is worth quoting:

> Therefore, we proclaime,
> If any spirit breathes within this round,
> Uncapable of waightie passion
> (As from his birth, being hugged in the armes,
> And nuzzled twixt the breastes of happinesse)
> Who winkes, and shuts his apprehension up
> From common sense of what men were, and are,
> Who would not knowe what men must be; let such
> Hurrie amaine from our black visag'd showes:
> We shall affright their eyes. But if a breast,
> Nail'd to the earth with griefe: if any heart
> Pierc't through with anguish, pant within this ring:
> If there be any blood, whose heate is choakt
> And stifled with true sense of misery:
> If ought of these straines fill this consort up,
> Th' arrive most welcome.

The implications are several: that this kind of drama is 'black visag'd', frightful; that its darkness corresponds to a darkness in actuality, not universally experienced but palpable to those who do not shut their apprehensions up "From common sense of what men were, and are", who in fact "knowe what men must be"; that the effect of the play is to be achieved only if there is in the spectator a pre-existent knowledge of this darkness. There is here no suggestion of a reforming value in the drama, only the idea that the audience will understand the dramatist's picture of life if their own is not unlike it. Marston gives us no coherent theory of the tragic, no comment on the nature of the tragic hero, no suggestion of a delicate balancing between pride in human nature and terror at the image of the world presented. No more than his greater successors in tragic drama had Marston worked out his ideas, but certainly this prologue points to a state of affairs in the minds of dramatic authors which led them to write tragically about this time, led them to seek the companionship of others whose breasts were "Nail'd to the earth with griefe", whose hearts were "Pierc't through with anguish" and whose natural warmth was "choakt And stifled with true sense of misery". The authors of *Lear* and *The Duchess of Malfi* and *Bussy d'Ambois* and even *Volpone* had become ready to slight those who had not known anguish, who from their birth had been "hugged in the armes, And nuzzled twixt the breastes of happinesse".

This preoccupation with an irredeemable darkness was the inevitable result of a weakening of faith. Dr. Tillyard has forced us to see that the Elizabethans held fast to a medieval cosmology, that their assumptions about 'degree' have a religious or magical basis; [1] and the pragmatism of Machiavelli, the scepticism of Montaigne introduced only modifications of an inherited pattern. Yet it is significant that the fullest dramatic expression of the notion of 'degree' comes in *Troilus and Cressida*, a play that Professor Ellis-Fermor has described as the consummate expression of an anarchic vision, a play which seems to show above all others the vanity of existence, the inherent sickness of human nature.[2] So full a formulation as Ulysses gives comes most naturally when the idea is no longer so potent in the minds of men: it is then made explicit, because it can no longer be taken for granted. Yet in the early seventeenth century 'degree' was still a powerful idea, and when Shakespeare wrote *Macbeth* he was with part of his mind intent on the evils that come from usurpation, the discord that sounds with the untuning of the string. Similarly in *Lear* he thought to some extent with Sackville and Norton in *Gorboduc*, tracing the ills of the kingdom and the royal house to the king's abandonment

---

[1] *The Elizabethan World Picture*, 1943; *Shakespeare's History Plays*, 1944.
[2] *The Frontiers of Drama*, pp. 56–76.

of power and his subjecting himself to his own children. But neither *Macbeth* nor *Lear* is primarily a political tract, as *Gorboduc* is. We have already seen the oddity that Chapman could speak of 'excitation to virtue, and deflection from her contrary' in relation to *The Revenge of Bussy d'Ambois*: in the same way, it is impossible for *Macbeth* to be a political tract, if the dramatist implies that the pattern of events is preordained. The insistence on the witches' most accurate foreknowledge of each step in the action puts the play into a different category from that of the histories. In Shakespeare's dramatisation of the historical events that preceded the establishment of the Tudor monarchy, he was issuing a warning against the recurrence of civil strife and usurpation: in *Lear* and *Macbeth* he shows the infringement of 'degree' as fated: it is as evil in its effects as before, but is now an ill to which the world is haphazardly subject. It is not so much the diseased will of one man or of a group that leads to the disturbance of order, but rather it is Fortune who infects the individual and the whole frame of things. Sometimes, indeed, the dramatist's pessimism goes further, as when Lear cries out against the existence of Goneril and Regan, with the question: "Is there any cause in Nature that makes these hard hearts?" (III. vi), or when he sees the ranks of society and the normal processes of human justice as based on nothing more substantial than chance:

> See how yond justice rails upon yon simple thief. Hark in thine ear: change places; and, handy-dandy, which is the justice, which is the thief? (IV. vi.)

In general, however, there remains a notion of an ideal order in Shakespearian tragedy, disrupted through action discordant with 'degree' but not originating simply in a human being's evil choice.

The change from the political morality of *Gorboduc* and

the histories to the determinist outlook of the tragedies was doubtless in part the fruit of change in the political scene and the social structure. In Elizabeth's last years there were intrigues in plenty for the succession. The Infanta of Spain, the Earl of Derby, Essex were among those who in the minds of many had claims as impressive as those that James VI could produce, and the fire which the Essex rebellion lit in the hearts of some must have scorched the paper on which the canons of 'degree' had been laboriously set out. And when James VI had inherited, it was no longer so easy to see magic in sovereignty: Elizabeth could be hated, but she had a magnetism and an isolation that James signally lacked, qualities that primacy seems naturally to demand. Moreover, society's change from the land-basis to the money-basis was becoming increasingly apparent. In Peele's *The Old Wives' Tale*, acted about 1592, the magician Sacrapant has conjured up a Friar, 'the veriest knave in all Spain', to entertain his fair captive Delia: when she asks the Friar: "Which is the most greediest Englishman?", the answer comes pat and without comment: "The miserable and most covetous usurer." In Greene's *James IV*, of about the same time, there is a scene (V. iv) which appears to have got into the play by accident, being merely a conversation between a Divine, a Lawyer and a Merchant on the bad condition of the time: as each of the three professions represented is blamed in turn, the debate is inconclusive, but its occurrence in the play suggests an increasing awareness that something was unhealthy in the social structure. There is an equally noticeable irrelevancy in *Romeo and Juliet*, acted about three years later, when Romeo buys' poison from the Apothecary and tells him that the gold he is parting with is more noxious than the mortal drug he is receiving (V. i). A year or two later, there is at least a kind of seriousness in *The Merchant of Venice* when we are

33   D

shown that the golden casket does not contain the prize
and that the usurer's trade can put a man's life in jeopardy.
But after the turn of the century the attacks on gold
become more virulent in the drama of the time. Lear and
Timon see it as the universal corrupter, the trafficker in
justice and honour; Volpone and Face lead men to their
undoing by holding up the gilded bait. But among the
metals gold had the primacy, as the lion among beasts, the
eagle among birds, the king among men. If gold was
corrupting and deceitful, men might come to see rottenness in other sovereign things, might come at last to question whether the hierarchies had been rightly conceived.
Such inchoate scepticism might well be directed towards
the political order, especially now that James was on the
throne, and in *Bussy d'Ambois* Chapman goes out of his
way to praise the court of Elizabeth as a model to Europe
and a contrast to the French court. King Henry says:

> Assure you, cousin Guise, so great a courtier,
> So full of majesty and royal parts,
> No queen in Christendom may vaunt herself.
> Her Court approves it, that's a Court indeed,
> Not mixt with clowneries used in common houses,
> But, as Courts should be, th' abstracts of their kingdoms,
> In all the beauty, state, and worth they hold,
> So is hers, amply, and by her inform'd.
> The world is not contracted in a man
> With more proportion and expression,
> Than in her Court, her kingdom. Our French Court
> Is a mere mirror of confusion to it:
> The king and subject, lord and every slave,
> Dance a continual hay; our rooms of state
> Kept like our stables; no place more observed
> Than a rude market-place.   (I. ii.)

He goes on to add that the English will soon realise the
difference if they change their court-form to one like

the French, and Monsieur, his brother, adds the sharp comment:

> No question we shall see them imitate
> (Though afar off) the fashions of our Courts,
> As they have ever aped us in attire.

This goes to the roots of things in a way that Spenser's satirical comments on court life do not, for Chapman's criticism by implication does not spare the ruler himself. Such criticism was not reserved for the temporal hierarchy: as tragedy was so often set in southern lands, the dramatists might consider themselves licensed to make free with Italianate cardinals, but often their thrusts have an anti-ecclesiastical direction. In *The Duchess of Malfi* the dramatist seems fully in sympathy with his Duchess when she asserts that her solemn exchange of vows with Antonio makes the formal blessing of the church supererogatory. "What can the church force more?" she asks, and later: "How can the church build faster? We now are man and wife, and 'tis the church That must but echo this." (I. i.) Towards the end of the play, the Cardinal says of Antonio: "Although he do account religion But a school-name" (V. ii), and our feeling is strengthened that Webster's world-picture is to a considerable extent antinomian. Not entirely so, for *The Duchess of Malfi*, like *Macbeth*, shows the dreadfulness that follows on a breaking with 'degree': Antonio and the Duchess have neglected the specialty of rule. But Webster's sympathy with them is far greater than his reprobation, and the dominant impression left by the play is that the hierarchies among men are unsound.

The goodness of the natural and the supernatural order was not the only article of faith available for an Elizabethan. There was too the typically Renaissance belief in the splendour of human life, that belief which dominates Italian painting and sculpture at its finest, which provides the motive-force for the early plays of Marlowe. Burck-hardt, in his *The Civilisation of the Renaissance in Italy*, makes us understand how in the fifteenth century men became imbued with a new consciousness of power, a keener delight in its employment. His account of Leon Battista Alberti should be one of the starting-points for a consideration of Jacobean tragedy, for the great peal that rings in Alberti's life is both dimly echoed and denied by Shakespeare and Chapman and Webster:

In all by which praise is won, Leon Battista was from his childhood the first. Of his various gymnastic feats and exercises we read with astonishment how, with his feet together, he could spring over a man's head; how, in the cathedral, he threw a coin in the air till it was heard to ring against the distant roof; how the wildest horses trembled under him. In three things he desired to appear faultless to others, in walking, in riding, and in speaking. He learned music without a master, and yet his compositions were admired by professional judges. Under the pressure of poverty, he studied both civil and canonical law for many years, till exhaustion brought on a severe illness. In his twenty-fourth year, finding his memory for words weakened, but his sense of facts unimpaired, he set to work at physics and mathematics. And all the while he acquired every sort of accomplishment and dexterity, cross-examining artists, scholars and artisans of all descriptions, down to the cobblers, about the secrets and peculiarities of their craft. Painting and modelling he practised by the way, and especially excelled in admirable likenesses from memory. Great admiration was excited by his mysterious 'camera obscura', in which he showed at one time the stars and the moon rising over rocky hills, and at another wide landscapes with mountains and gulfs receding into dim perspective, and with fleets advancing on the waters in shade or sunshine. And that which others created he welcomed joyfully, and held every human achievement which followed the laws of beauty for something almost divine. To all this must be added his literary works, first of all those on art, which are landmarks and authorities of the first order for the Renaissance of Form, especially in architecture; then his Latin prose writings—novels and other works—of which some have been taken for productions of antiquity; his elegies, eclogues, and humorous dinner-speeches. He also wrote an Italian treatise on domestic life in four books; and even a funeral oration on his dog. His serious and witty sayings were thought worth collecting, and specimens of them, many columns long, are quoted in his biography. And all that he had and knew he imparted, as rich natures always do, without the least reserve, giving away his chief discoveries for nothing. But the deepest spring of his nature has yet to be spoken of— the sympathetic intensity with which he entered into the whole life around him. At the sight of noble trees and waving corn-fields he shed tears; handsome and dignified old men he honoured as 'a delight of nature', and could never look at them enough. Perfectly formed animals won his goodwill as being specially favoured by nature; and more than once, when he was ill, the sight of a beautiful landscape cured him. No wonder that those who saw him in this close and mysterious communion with the world ascribed to him the gift of prophecy. He was said to have foretold a bloody catastrophe in the family of Este, the fate of Florence, and the death of the Popes years before they happened, and to be able to read into the countenances and the hearts of men. It need not be added that an iron will pervaded and sustained his whole personality; like all the great men of the Renaissance, he said: "Men can do all things if they will."

And Leonardo da Vinci was to Alberti as the finisher to the beginner, as the master to the *dilettante*. Would only that Vasari's work were here supplemented by a description like that of Alberti! The colossal outlines of Leonardo's nature can never be more than dimly and distantly conceived.[1]

That this underlies *Tamburlaine* is at once obvious: the delights and the ambitions of Alberti come to be Tamburlaine's appetite for greatness, for splendour of setting and the homage of men, for the divine Zenocrate, for riding in triumph through Persepolis, for the sweet fruition of an earthly crown, for recognition as the scourge of God. And

[1] Jacob Burckhardt, *The Civilisation of the Renaissance*, 1944, pp. 86–7.

if we find some coarseness of temper in Tamburlaine's dreams, that is not surprising. The Elizabethan playhouse, the Reformation, the formulation of practical politics that we associate with Machiavelli—these all united in taking away from the Renaissance temper something of fineness. And perhaps because the dream of human greatness was less golden, was snatched from under the eyes of the reformers, was with difficulty harnessed with a delight in political intrigue, was expressed in the still primitive theatrical terms of the 1580's, it was less enduring than Italy had known it. Even in *Tamburlaine* itself, the defection of Calyphas in Part II, his wanton truancy from his father's battles, raises awkward questions. His preference for a game of cards over witnessing yet another of his father's victories is so obviously sensible when the spectators themselves have been sated with Tamburlaine's long line of triumphs; his brutal execution at his father's hands therefore seems to hint that Marlowe was growing weary of his own dream, would be ill-content with a repetition. If *Faustus* is Marlowe's next play, it is significant that there the aspirations of the individual are given to us in a morality-framework, that there is an uneasy balance between orthodoxy of religious belief and antinomianism. Later Marlowe was to turn to the more orthodox view of things, and in *Edward II*, *The Jew of Malta* and *The Massacre at Paris* there are many assertions of the sacredness of 'degree': the thirst for power is shown in the Jew and Mortimer and the Guise only to be reprobated. It is as if Marlowe had at least partially abandoned the worship of man for the worship of divine decree.

But if the splendour of earthly aspiration grew tarnished in Marlowe's hands, it was indeed a crumbling idol for the Jacobeans. Chapman's Bussy tells us that advancement comes because it must and not because we will it, that great place brings greater vulnerability and closer contact with the antics of the court; Jonson parodies the Renaissance man in Sir Epicure Mammon; men are the stars' tennis-balls, flies at the mercy of the wanton gods, asses to be led by the nose, players strutting at the playwright's beck, bodies that rot into dust and souls driven in a black storm. Yet, just as the notion of 'degree' underlies the Jacobean cosmology, so the Renaissance dream of greatness is the necessary foundation for the tragic heroes of the time. The dramatists inherited a cult of stoicism from Seneca, but it is not for their imperturbability that we admire Lear and Othello and Hamlet: in the end, it is true, they learn to stand up to Fortune's blows and to go out with dignity and a conventional gesture of resignation; but we must remember that Macbeth dies in despair, Othello in terrible remorse, and Lear with his nerves stretched beyond breaking-point by his hope that Cordelia may yet live. It is not so much their capacity for endurance as their sharp sense of their own being that marks them out as exceptional. Hamlet, Lear and Macbeth come to greater self-knowledge, and Hamlet throughout the play has the many-sidedness of the typical Renaissance figure: he is the scholar, the expert with his rapier, the connoisseur of the stage, the poet too, and likely, had he been put on, to have proved most royally. If Othello has not the self-knowledge of the others, he has at least a superabundance of vitality, he exults in his power, his eloquence, his animal vigour, his regality of gesture to the very end. Even for Jonson the Renaissance dream was not entirely dead: he was fascinated by the aspiring Sejanus and Catiline, though he hated them too, and he could show the fascination of power and sensuality in Volpone while at the same time giving him the comic shiftiness of the fox and bringing him at last into fetters.

As we pass beyond the first decade of the seventeenth century, we find that the Jacobean scepticism becomes ultimately destructive of tragedy. Major works of literature seem to depend on a tension between two ways of perception. We have seen that, according to Professor Ellis-Fermor, there is in tragedy an equilibrium set up by the opposition of a divine and an anthropocentric interpretation of the universe: the tragic writer is as it were wrestling with his salvation before ultimately surrendering to it.[1] This would seem to be a simplification, for *Macbeth* and *Othello* hardly suggest the notion of a benevolent overseer. But there appears to be in Jacobean tragedy a state of balance between a conception of the universe as order and a conception of the universe as chaos, between the notion of man's dignity and the notion of his insignificance. When the equilibrium is destroyed, the movement may be towards a despair of order and dignity, as in *Timon of Athens*, or towards a reassertion of traditional beliefs, as in Shirley's *St. Patrick for Ireland*. In the drama that followed the short period of great tragedy, we have the drama of indifference, as in Beaumont and Fletcher and their followers, the conventionally built but fundamentally unthoughtful drama of Massinger, and the approach to complete antinomianism in Ford. Life has become a languid pageant of woe in *The Broken Heart*, and it requires the fierce rebelliousness of Giovanni to bring back the tension once again: in one Caroline play, *'Tis Pity She's a Whore*, we thus recapture the Jacobean equilibrium, but tragedy recovers like a spent taper, for a flash, and instantly goes out. The nullity of Caroline tragedy as a whole is forcibly illustrated in Shirley's *The Cardinal*, the last tragedy to be acted before the Civil War: it is a competent piece of work in its kind, but the mechanical approach of the dramatist is shown in his

[1] Cf. above, p. 7.

frequent echoes of Jacobean writing, and in his picture of the villainous Cardinal. There would be a piquancy in the drawing of such an ecclesiastical villain by James Shirley, a convert to the Church of Rome, were it not that we feel how derivative the portrait is. In seventeenth-century drama cardinals had become traditionally fair game, and the play did not mean enough to Shirley for him to make it consonant with his new allegiance. The Cardinal dies echoing Vittoria Corombona:

> now it would be rare,—
> If you but waft me with a little prayer;
> My wings that flag may catch the wind; but 'tis
> In vain, the mist is risen, and there's none
> To steer my wandering bark.   (V. iii.)

and the difference of the wording makes us realise again that Shirley is following a dramatic pattern rather than communicating a personal vision. Orthodoxy, indifference, and something very close to unbelief itself, can all be found in the later Jacobean and Caroline plays, but except momentarily in Ford there was not the balancing of belief and scepticism, of order and chaos, of human splendour and corruption.

But in another way we find an equilibrium of forces in Jacobean tragedy. On the other hand, there is a strong sense of determinism, as we have seen; on the other, the characters have that degree of lifelikeness that makes it seem always possible for them to exercise free will. Here, indeed, we touch on one of the problems of tragic writing: the dramatist is presenting a picture of the world in which man is subject to the operations of cosmic forces, blind or purposive, and cannot carve out his own future. But if he is merely one of the stars' tennis-balls, it is difficult to see how we can preserve an idea of his dignity: if he is a manipulated doll, the world becomes something between a

Bartholomew Fair and a *Walpurgisnacht*. In sixteenth-century drama the foreordaining of event is heavily underlined. Material from historical sources lent itself to this kind of handling, for the development of the action was necessarily determined by the actual sequence of events, and in plays with entirely fictional plots the dramatist would go out of his way to make us realise that the end was settled simultaneously with the beginning: in *The Spanish Tragedy* the presence of Andrea's Ghost and Revenge throughout the play serves as a permanent assurance that revenge will be accomplished; in *Romeo and Juliet* the initial chorus foretells the love and its doom; in *James IV* and *The Old Wives' Tale* the use of the induction makes it clear that what is being presented belongs already to the past and is therefore settled in its every detail. The use of the induction is, indeed, highly significant in the development of dramatic technique at this time, and we must later examine it from that angle: for the moment we shall notice it as underlining the powerlessness of the dramatic characters to change the course of events. But in none of these plays is the tragic spirit fully apparent: there is sensational incident, and an occasional touch of that darkness of experience which Marston speaks of in his prologue to *Antonio's Revenge*; but we get neither the notion of human greatness in adversity nor the long persistence of terror. In *Tamburlaine*, indeed, there are latent the forces that in tragedy balance one another, but that play is so brimmed with eloquence, so pageant-like a series of triumphs, until the end, that the tragic problem is there unobtrusive. In Jacobean drama, on the other hand, we have a kind of dual vision of the action: simultaneously it appears foreordained and dependent on the characters' choice. Only in *Macbeth* among the great tragedies does Shakespeare labour the idea of predestination, and even there Macbeth and his wife are drawn so convincingly as human beings that, as in actuality, it appears always that freedom of choice exists even though we may have decided that the overall pattern is not of our making. In Greek tragedy the events are decreed, the reactions of the characters are free. In Shakespeare and the best of his contemporaries, action is not separated from thought and feeling: each is fore-ordained, yet each seems always a new birth. We feel simultaneously that Desdemona is doomed and that she may escape, that Macbeth's sin is decreed and that the temptation could be resisted, that Lear must die and that Edmund's repentance may come in time.

One cannot say that the tragedies that followed the great ones are characterised by a one-sided stress on free will. The later writers modelled themselves too closely on their predecessors to forgo the generally fatalistic air. But at least the tragicomedies in the Beaumont and Fletcher style illustrate well enough the breakdown of this equilibrium too. *A King and No King* is only the most notorious example of a haphazard putting of things to rights: the action seems destined for disaster until the last act, when an unexpected revelation offers a fortunate con-clusion. When Edmund Waller in the late seventeenth century altered *The Maid's Tragedy* and gave that too a happy ending,[1] he was only making the play consistent with others of its kind: if Arbaces can escape his doom, there seems no reason for Amintor to suffer. The situation is rather different in Shakespeare's romances, when we have the suggestion that a providence safeguards the main characters from ultimate harm: this, however, is a return to the earlier stressing of predestination. Only in the major tragedies, those of the great decade, is the balance preserved.

I have tried to suggest certain features of the picture of

[1] Cf. below, p. 108.

the world seen by the early seventeenth-century tragic writers. Standing between a belief in natural order and a growing perception of chaos, between the Renaissance enthusiasm for living and an ever-darkening disillusion, between the twin poles of Fate and Chance, of predestination and free will, they went through mental experiences of a peculiar intensity, knew the darkness and the terror all the more keenly for the light that still remained in a diminishing fragment of the heavens. And because their feelings were so deeply stirred by the contradictions in their experience, they were led to the writing of tragic literature. It was almost coincidental that this should be the time when the development of playhouse technique had made tragic drama possible. Until around 1595 the dramatic medium was insufficiently subtle, and after 1615 or thereabouts it had acquired characteristics which made great tragedy far more difficult to achieve. That second major reason for the brevity of the tragic period I wish to examine next. Even without the change in technique, however, the tragic world-view would not have lasted long. A delicate equilibrium is soon gone when the winds of heaven blow, and because the tragic dramatists of James's time were barely conscious of their own aims, the equilibrium was precarious indeed.

Chapter 3

THE TRAGIC STYLE

D E QUINCEY, writing in 1840 on the theory of
Greek tragedy, tried to make his readers understand
the Greek way of dramatic writing by instituting a comparison between that style and the one used by Elizabethan tragic authors for a play-within-the-play. When
Shakespeare is giving us the words and actions of Hamlet
and Claudius and Gertrude, he is presenting to us something not far removed from the kind of life that we
ourselves experience, though the presentation, says De
Quincey, is 'exalted' and 'selected'; but our attitude to
the characters in the play we are seeing is paralleled by the
attitude of those characters to the Player-King and Player-
Queen in *The Murder of Gonzago*.[1] The play itself is once-
removed from us, the play-within-the-play twice-removed.
Consequently Shakespeare in *Hamlet* uses a very different
style in the inserted play, and incidentally in the quoted
passages about Hecuba, from the style which he thought
appropriate to the rest of *Hamlet*. The style of *The Murder
of Gonzago* is heavily stylised, made stiff with conventional
figures and ornaments, the lines are in rhyme, the characters declaim at one another or at the audience. The
contrast between all this and the interruptions of Hamlet
and the courtiers makes the one style appear less naturalistic
and the other more naturalistic than by itself it would. When
we hear the Player-Queen promising fidelity in this way:

> Nor earth to me give food, nor heaven light!
> Sport and repose lock from me day and night!

---

[1] "Theory of Greek Tragedy" (*The Collected Writings of Thomas De
Quincey*, edited by David Masson, 1897, x. 344–5).

To desperation turn my trust and hope!
An anchor's cheer in prison be my scope!
Each opposite that blanks the face of joy
Meet what I would have well, and it destroy!
Both here and hence pursue me lasting strife,
If, once a widow, ever I be wife!   (III. ii.)

it is Hamlet's "If she should break it now!" that emphasises the theatrical contrivance of the speech. In itself, it is no more obviously artificial than the famous words of Hieronimo, first spoken some dozen years before in *The Spanish Tragedy*:

Oh eies, no eies, but fountains fraught with teares;
Oh life, no life, but liuely fourme of death;
O world, no world, but masse of publique wrongs,
Confusde and filde with murder and misdeeds.
O sacred heauens, if this vnhallowed deed,
If this inhumane and barberous attempt,
If this incomparable murder thus
Of mine, but now no more my sonne,
Shall vnreueald and vnrevenged passe,
How should we tearme your dealings to be iust,
If you vniustly deale with those, that in your iustice
   trust?   (III. ii.)

What Shakespeare has done, in fact, is simply to go back to a dramatic style that not long before had been customary for serious writing, a style in which Senecan rhetoric and over-regular verse strained towards high astounding terms. When that earlier style was momentarily brought back, as in a play-within-the-play or by means of a burlesque quotation, the development which the passage of a dozen years had seen was accentuated. "Go by, Jeronimo!" and "Holla, ye pampered jades of Asia!" were lines always good for a laugh, out of their original contexts.

But it was a development of style, and not a sudden change, that took place in the 1590's. If we turn from the beginning of *Dr. Faustus* to the beginning of *Othello*, we seem to have left one dramatic world for another: the long expository speech of Faustus, who sums up his search for knowledge and his growing inclination towards forbidden things, in a language as obviously contrived as a public orator's Latin, is far away indeed from the almost casual interchanges of Iago and Roderigo, who seem to speak without preparation, letting their thoughts and feelings jostle one another in the utterance. But if we turn back a few years from *Othello* to *Hamlet* we find the new tragic style not nearly so fully developed. Mr. T. S. Eliot has drawn our attention to the different kinds of verse that can be found in this earliest of the great tragedies.[1] This, he says, is like *Romeo and Juliet*:

> But, look, the morn is russet mantle clad,
> Walks o'er the dew of yon high eastern hill;   (I. i.)

while this, in contrast, belongs to Shakespeare's most mature verse-style:

> Up from my cabin,
> My sea-gown scarf'd about me, in the dark
> Grop'd I to find out them, had my desire,
> Finger'd my packet.   (V. ii.)

More recently Mr. Salvador de Madariaga has made some interesting deductions from those passages in *Hamlet* which are written in the earlier style. He takes the King's address to the court in I. ii:

> Therefore our sometime sister, now our queen,
> The imperial jointress of this war-like state,
> Have we, as 'twere with a defeated joy,
> With one auspicious and one dropping eye,

---

[1] *Selected Essays*, pp. 143–4.

> With mirth in funeral and with dirge in marriage,
> In equal scale weighing delight and dole,
> Taken to wife;

and argues that Shakespeare was here, as it were, burlesquing his own theme. "Obviously," he says, "this is not what such a king at such a moment should say. Shakespeare himself, beholding the sight from above the play, struck by its balance and poise between joy and grief, writes those see-saw lines, thoroughly amused by *them*, and not caring a rap for—or forgetting—the likelihood of it all." [1] And Mr. Madariaga blames Shakespeare for a 'certain lack of measure, a bombast, an exaggeration', a readiness 'to pander to the worst tastes of the crowd', which he says is evident in the famous lines: [2]

> 'Tis now the very witching time of night,
> When churchyards yawn and hell itself breathes out
> Contagion to this world: now could I drink hot blood,
> And do such bitter business as the day
> Would quake to look on.   (III. ii.)

But Mr. Madariaga tends to see the play out of its theatrical context. It was written about two years later than Marston's *Antonio's Revenge*, where we can read this:

> 'Tis yet dead night, yet al the earth is cloucht
> In the dull leaden hand of snoring sleepe:
> No breath disturbs the quiet of the ayre.
> No spirit moves upon the breast of earth,
> Save howling dogs, nightcrowes, and screeching owls,
> Save meager ghosts, *Piero*, and black thoughts.   (I. i.)

Marston himself is far away from Kyd in the general temper of his work, and in the prevailing manner of his dramatic speech. But throughout the period Hieronimo and Andronicus and Tamburlaine were popular figures of

---

[1] *On Hamlet*, 1948, p. 122.   [2] *Ibid.*, p. 127.

the stage, and their rhetorical violence was not to be easily outgrown. Shakespeare, indeed, can be seen passing from the earlier style to the later in his sequence of history plays. Richard III is a cousin of Marlowe's heroes and speaks their tongue: he could not exist in the same play as Falstaff. Yet at the end of the sequence of plays, *Henry V* is not without its flourishes of speech, and the newly made royalty at the end of *Henry IV* plays with antithesis and a theatrical affectation when he addresses his brothers on the subject of his father's death:

> This new and gorgeous garment, majesty,
> Sits not so easy on me as you think.
> Brothers, you mix your sadness with some fear:
> This is the English, not the Turkish court;
> Not Amurath an Amurath succeeds,
> But Harry Harry. . . .
> For me, by heaven, I bid you be assur'd,
> I'll be your father and your brother too;
> Let me but bear your love, I'll bear your cares:
> Yet weep that Harry's dead, and so will I;
> But Harry lives that shall convert those tears
> By number into hours of happiness.   (V. ii.)

So in *Hamlet* we can find a passage of stichomythia, where the thrust and parry of the lines is much in the Kyd style:

> *Queen.* Hamlet, thou hast thy father much offended.
> *Hamlet.* Mother, you have my father much offended.
> *Queen.* Come, come, you answer with an idle tongue.
> *Hamlet.* Go, go, you question with a wicked tongue.
> (III. iv.)

Yet this is the exordium to a scene where mother and son speak so intimately and without the restraints of a formal-ised expression.

We find, then, that by the beginning of the seventeenth century the development of dramatic speech had brought a naturalness of utterance that makes us think of the men and women of the plays as speaking without preparation, as indeed living their lives in front of us at the theatre. Though we know that we are seeing actors on a stage, uttering lines set down for them, lines learned by heart and rehearsed, we can at the same time regard them as if they were speaking directly from their hearts. That this was not the case for earlier audiences, when they saw Hieronimo and Hamlet's other predecessors, is apparent from the highly formalised framework of the earlier plays. I have already suggested that the devices of prologue and induction and inter-act comment prevent such plays as *The Spanish Tragedy* and *James IV* from being taken as other than contrived pageants, more or less formal illustrations of a governing idea. Though the secularisation of the drama had proceeded a great way by the time of the University Wits, yet their plays still had the nature of a ritual. The prologue to Thomas Preston's *Cambises* tells us of the duties of kingship, and of the fate that lies in store for the delinquent monarch; the play that follows is little more than a demonstration of the truth of this initial proposition; the epilogue fittingly prays for the Queen. Kyd is more sophisticated than Preston, but we have seen that the presence of Don Andrea and Revenge, as spectators of the drama, similarly gives the whole action a ritual cast. Both induction and prologue are common in the last decade of the sixteenth century, but then seem to fall into comparative disuse. Shakespeare's seventeenth-century plays are commonly printed without prologues, many of the prologues and epilogues in the Beaumont and Fletcher folios are obviously Caroline additions, and Massinger in his dedication to *The Unnatural Combat*, acted about 1621 but not printed until 1639, explains the absence of prologue and epilogue by saying that the play was 'composed at a time . . . when such by-ornaments were not advanced above the fabric of the whole work'.

The induction, which we find early in *James IV*, *The Old Wives' Tale* and *The Taming of the Shrew*, acquired a new lease of life around the turn of the century. *Antonio and Mellida*, *The Malcontent*, *Every Man Out of his Humour* and *Cynthia's Revels* all give us examples of the induction as a vehicle for theatrical comment: we are, as it were, taken into the green-room, introduced to the actors, and made to approach the play through a prior acquaintance with them. As indeed we were, though without dialogue, in the film version of *Henry V*. Marston and Jonson found the device useful for shrewd tilting with their rivals in the theatre, but I think the reason for its use lies deeper. In such plays as *Antonio and Mellida* and *The Malcontent* and even in the Jonson comedies, the playwrights felt it necessary to lead the audience by degrees to the world of the play itself, they were more or less conscious of the gulf that separated the spectator from the dramatic characters, the language and experience of common life from the dialect and traffic of the stage. When, however, a more naturalistic way of writing had come with, approximately, the new century, the induction was no longer a needed stepping-stone and thus almost disappeared from English drama. It has, however, been noted by Mr. J. M. Nosworthy that in *Hamlet* Shakespeare uses the scenes with Hamlet and the players very much in the fashion of Marston and Jonson with their inductions.[1] In *Hamlet* there is comment on the ways of acting, on the theatre-war between the children's companies and the adult players, and on the true function of the drama. But, instead of putting it at the beginning, Shakespeare spreads this induction material through the middle of his play, holding up the action, indeed, but at the same time throwing further light on the Prince's

[1] "The Structural Experiment in *Hamlet*" (*The Review of English Studies*, xxii (1946), 281–6).

character, emphasising the extent of his deviation from the path of duty, and not making the theatrical criticism and comment a kind of bar which the audience must cross before coming to the play itself. We have a device similar to an induction in M. Jean-Paul Sartre's *Crime Passionel*, where the play is a representation of the events that are being recalled and narrated by the chief character: most spectators would probably agree that, in a comparatively naturalistic play, we feel cheated when we are made to shift from one series of happenings to another which belongs to a different time-sequence and which, because it belongs already to the past, has a too obviously pre-determined outcome. So we should resent an induction to *Hamlet*, and it is significant that Shakespeare transferred the induction material to within the body of the play. *Hamlet* is in itself sufficiently close to us in its language and its rhythm of event to need no footbridge. *Antonio and Mellida*, however, needed as firm riveting to the outside world as an induction could give it.

We can assume, I think, that the earliest years of the seventeenth century saw a new kind of atmosphere in the playhouse, one in which the spectators felt an immediacy in the action of the drama, an actuality in the characters and their speech. They no longer went to see a woeful or comic pageant unfolded before their eyes, they went rather to see things happen—though admittedly they knew well enough, with part of their minds, that the pattern of event and the choice of words were dictated by the dramatist. And that was possible because the new style of theatrical language was sufficiently close to real life for the spectator to accept it as the not impossible utterance of a man speaking unprompted. There would be some set speeches, it is true, like Othello's farewell to his occupation or Lear's formal cursing of his eldest daughter, but these would come at moments of such emotional tension that the credulity of the audience would be heightened, its suggestibility increased. Through the play as a whole, with a free use of prose for informal speech and a blank verse which rarely obtruded its regular shape, the atmosphere would stay close to actuality—far closer, anyway, than the sixteenth-century dramatists had ever imagined.

In his introduction to the Tudor Translations edition of Seneca, Mr. Eliot has pointed to one important difference between the Senecan and the Elizabethan drama.[1] Though both delighted in rhetoric, in violence of imagery and description, though both found stoicism a refuge, they are seen to be remote from each other when we consider the purely narrative interest of Elizabethan plays. We and Seneca's côterie-audience know in advance the story of Thyestes or Hercules, but the spectator of *Othello* or *A Woman Killed with Kindness* is anxious to find out what is going to happen as the play proceeds: the dramatist may give him a general idea of the pattern of event, but his curiosity will be aroused as to the exact development of Iago's scheming, and indeed in Heywood's case the ending can hardly be guessed. But to this we must add that narrative-interest becomes much more powerful around the turn of the century than it was before. We have seen that plays like *Cambises* and *Faustus* have little of it, and it is only when we have a sense of the action playing itself out independently before our eyes that we begin to feel anxious concerning its outcome. But again it must be emphasised that no sudden change took place: there was some narrative-interest in *Friar Bacon and Friar Bungay*, some even in *Tamburlaine*, far more in Marston, and far less in Shakespeare than in most dramatists born later.

Now if we turn from the tragedies of the great decade to the plays that succeeded them—the tragicomedies of

---

[1] *Seneca His Tenne Tragedies* (The Tudor Translations, New Series), 1927, i. xxv–vi.

Beaumont and Fletcher and their imitators, the tragedies of Middleton and Massinger—we find that the tendencies already noticed have continued to operate. The blank verse of, say, 1620–42 is less obviously metrical than Shakespeare's or Jonson's; the language of the later Jacobean and the Caroline plays is far closer to that of common life than is ever the case in Shakespearian tragedy; in some comedies, indeed, prose becomes the dominant medium. Middleton's *The Changeling* gives an excellent example of the later tragic style. Beatrice-Joanna and De Flores are figures cast in the mould that Shakespeare and Webster had used, yet neither of them has that gift of image-laden speech that Vittoria and Iago have as a natural right. Beatrice's speech to De Flores when she discovers that she is the price he puts on his services is characteristic of what we can call 'prose tragedy':

> Why, 'tis impossible thou canst be so wicked,
> Or shelter such a cunning cruelty,
> To make his death the murderer of my honour!
> Thy language is so bold and vicious,
> I cannot see which way I can forgive it
> With any modesty.   (III. iv.)

This is far from the language of *Measure for Measure*, a play of similar darkness and with an atmosphere close in many ways to Middleton's, where Claudio can thus reproach Isabella for holding back the news that he must die:

> Why give you me this shame?
> Think you I can a resolution fetch
> From flowery tenderness? If I must die,
> I will encounter darkness as a bride,
> And hug it in mine arms.   (III. i.)

and where his words on death, spoken soon after, are ever memorable:

Ay, but to die, and go we know not where;
To lie in cold obstruction and to rot;
This sensible warm motion to become
A kneaded clod . . . (III. i.)

Indeed, the prosifying of later blank verse is brought clearly home to us if we compare these passages with the following interchanges in Fletcher's *Thierry and Theodoret*, acted about 1616. Thierry is telling his beloved Ordella that he has vowed to kill her:

> *Thierry.* 'Tis terrible.
> *Ordella.* 'Tis so much the more noble.
> *Thierry.* 'Tis full of fearful shadows.
> *Ordella.* So is sleep, Sir.
> Or any thing that's meerly ours, and mortal,
> We were begotten gods else; but those fears
> Feeling but once the fires of nobler thoughts,
> Flie, like the shapes of clouds we form, to nothing.
>   *Thierry.* Suppose it death.
>   *Ordella.* I do.
>   *Thierry.* And endless parting
> With all we can call ours, with all our sweetness,
> With youth, strength, pleasure, people, time, nay reason:
> For in the silent grave, no conversation,
> No joyful tread of friends, no voice of Lovers,
> No careful Fathers counsel, nothing's heard,
> Nor nothing is, but all oblivion,
> Dust and an endless darkness, and dare you woman
> Desire this place ? (IV. i.)

We must note that the plane of converse is a lower one, that the images are less sharply defined than before, and there is no longer a moving economy of words. Attention has often been given to the growing frequency of extra-metrical syllables in Fletcherian blank verse, but that tendency needs to be linked with the decay in concrete imagery. The later characters speak with the blurred outlines of common speech: they do not appear, like Hotspur and Hamlet and Othello and so many other Shakespearian characters, as if every one of them were a poet. In the verse of Shakespeare's immediate successors we have an anticipation of the serious drama in prose that flourished in the earliest years of the present century. It is in many ways a far cry from *Thierry and Theodoret* and *The Changeling* to *Strife* and *Waste,* yet the reasons why we feel that the tragic experience is hardly given to us by Galsworthy and Granville Barker apply very similarly to Fletcher and Middleton. In prose or in blank verse which is not manifestly and authoritatively metrical, we can hardly feel that sense of verbal grandeur which seems necessary if the tragic character is to command our admiration and to speak fittingly for his and our kind.

Moreover, drama without eloquence lacks the ritual tone which we have seen most evident in the earliest drama but which to a considerable extent remained in the tragedies of the great decade. If the liturgical plays and *Everyman* and *Cambises* and *Faustus* are ceremonial illustrations of a proposition's validity, later tragic drama becomes a documentation of unhappy events. There are few cosmic implications in *The Changeling* or *Women Beware Women,* so that we feel that even Middleton's basic assumptions are hardly perceptible. We cannot say that the absence of fine speech caused the tendency towards mere documentation, or that the increasingly documentary purpose led to a prosifying of the language: rather we must see the two things as related symptoms. In the fifty years from about 1575 to about 1625 the drama changed from a clearly ritual form to a predominantly documentary form: ritual needs a faith to provide it with purpose, and it needs impressive utterance to make its effect. We have seen how the sixteenth-century basic assumptions were being modified at the beginning of the seventeenth century, how in the first decade there was in men's minds a state of tension, a transient equilibrium between belief and disbelief, and how thereafter there was an absence of tension because the dramatists no longer sufficiently cared. The Bulgarian scholar Dr. Marco Mincoff has recently published a paper on *Baroque Literature in England*, in which he has argued that we should take the Beaumont and Fletcher plays as the starting-point of English dramatic baroque.[1] Continental categories like 'Renaissance' and 'Baroque' do not lend themselves too readily to a study of English literature, for so much of our sixteenth- and seventeenth-century writing resists easy classification, but it is worth noting that Dr. Mincoff finds it necessary to employ a third term to cover work that comes in point of time between the 'Renaissance' and 'Baroque' styles. He speaks of 'the Revolt', a movement against the conventional Elizabethan, neo-petrarchan style and spirit, and here he places Donne, the later Shakespeare, Webster, Ben Jonson and the other major figures of the early Jacobean years. The term 'Revolt' is not altogether happy, for it implies, I think, too conscious a rejection of earlier assumptions and methods. We must remember that *Troilus and Cressida* contains the fullest assertion of the notion of 'degree', that Donne violently proclaims his orthodoxy of belief, that *Lear* includes frequent asseverations of divine justice. What is, however, indubitable is that these writers represent a state of tension, and reiterate their inheritance of belief all the more strongly because their hold on it is increasingly insecure. And so their utterance has not liturgical authority or the mighty line of human self-assurance: it has a new urgency as they look the cosmic problem in the face, a new concreteness of image as they seize on sense-impressions which are made

---

[1] *Baroque Literature in England* (Annuaire de l'Université de Sofia, Faculté Historico-Philologique, tome XLIII), 1947.

more vivid by their condition of mental excitement, and they retain something of the old eloquence not merely because they are the heirs of the immediate past but because at times the universe is still a splendidly ordered creation and because at other times the splendour is man's, the prerogative of the one kind of being that can suffer and comprehend its suffering.

And because the ritual motive was increasingly slight, the attention of the dramatists and of the audience was turned more and more to the narrative-interest of the play. In comedies and tragicomedies some influence of the Spanish cloak-and-sword drama is apparent, and in all the plays of Beaumont and Fletcher we are made to speculate freely on how things will in the end turn out. The last-act surprise, so notoriously evident in *A King and No King*, is a growing preoccupation with later Jacobean and Caroline dramatists. Again we must see the drama of the great decade as occupying a mid-position. Our interest in the story of *Macbeth* is sufficient to hold our attention firmly, but we are not so given over to speculation on the possible sequence of events that we have no leisure for contemplation of the play as a whole statement. Because from near the beginning we can see the outline of the completed action, we are made to feel its tragic implications throughout. If, on the other hand, we are for ever puzzling out who is the father of whom, for ever guessing more or less inaccurately who is the rightful ruler of the imaginary country we have been transported to, we shall not be concerned with any possible cosmic implications.

Professor Gerald Bentley has pointed out how important was the move of the King's Men to the Blackfriars Theatre towards the end of the great decade.[1] As the century progresses, the Blackfriars and the other 'private'

[1] "Shakespeare and the Blackfriars Theatre" (*Shakespeare Survey*, i (1948), 38–50).

theatres provide the setting for an increasing proportion of the more literate drama. Their audience was not the cross-section of the people of London that the Globe knew. It was altogether more genteel, with close contacts with court-circles. Not so narrow yet as it was to become in Restoration years, it was already approaching a gathering of social intimates. If we read a number of the prologues and epilogues written for private-theatre plays during Charles I's reign, we must be astonished at the likeness to Restoration manners in the picture of playhouse-behaviour provided by these informal comments. The fine clothes of the gentlemen; the smiles of the ladies, those 'high commissioners of wit' as Shirley calls them in his prologue to *The Coronation*, acted in 1635; the use of the playhouse for the contrivance of assignations; the intimate way in which the prologue-speaker addressed the seated gentry—all these things emerge again and again in the Caroline prologues and epilogues. It is not surprising that the dramatists, remembering their predecessors, were sometimes uncomfortably aware that the dramatic manner had changed. The actor Theophilus Bird, in his prologue to Ford's *The Ladies Triall* of 1638, laments that "The Muses chatter, who were wont to sing." Indeed the private playhouse was no likely setting for other than a gentlemanly, informal mode of speech.

The prologues and epilogues of these later years were very different in tone from those of the sixteenth century. The earlier examples we have seen were a means of bridging the gap between the audience and the theatricalised action, like the opening choral passage in *Murder in the Cathedral* or the long speech which begins *The Ascent of F6* —as it were, statements of the proposition which the coming ritual was to illustrate. The early tone was aloof, impersonal, and the matter of the prologue had a direct reference to what was to follow, as in the prologues to

Tamburlaine and *Romeo and Juliet*. The Caroline prologues, on the other hand, are intimate in tone, and their
subject-matter was often so unconnected with the play that
followed that the same prologue could be used for more
than one play. The prologue's function is then only to get
the audience into a friendly mood, to break a preliminary
jest as to-day an experienced lecturer may do before he
begins his discourse. While in the sixteenth century a
prologue-speaker emphasised the remoteness of the
dramatic action, his Caroline descendant was anxious only
to make the audience feel at home.

Yet of course there was one type of dramatic fare in the
Jacobean and Caroline years which was of a predominantly
ritual character. The masque's ceremonial pattern was
clear and invariable: however many antimasques might
precede, there was always the sequence of presenter's
speech, masquing-dance, revels and going-out song.
Moreover, each masque would have its theme, usually
indicated in its scenic framework, so that the whole entertainment proclaimed its end as the exalting of chastity or
love or the triumph of Britannia or peace. Rhyming verse,
fantastic scenes, magical devices removed the action from
common life. And with the masques we must remember
the court pastorals so beloved of Henrietta Maria. In *The
Shepherd's Paradise* of 1633 and the *Florimène* of 1635 we
have court plays which are as far away from the actual as
can be imagined: pseudo-Platonic ramblings on love, an
absurd disregard of the non-genteel in the earlier play,
spectacle and dance and the procession of the seasons in
the later, link up these pastorals with the masques, as
indeed did the presence of the Queen as chief actress in
The Shepherd's Paradise and as general supervisor of the
production of *Florimène*. Yet these masques and court
plays exhibit more clearly than anything else the intellectual bankruptcy of the later Jacobean and Caroline

drama. Only when ideas had become toys could such empty extravagance of homage be offered. At Kenilworth and Cowdray and Elvetham Elizabeth had been lavishly entertained, but the rites of her court seem securely based on a belief in the necessity of her sovereignty: the note is not forced there, any more than it is in the patriotic outbursts of the University Wits or of Shakespeare in his histories. Of all the seventeenth-century masques, only *Comus* gives the impression of conveying an idea that was other than a fashionable toy or a nostalgic fancy, and *Comus* was conceived and played far from Whitehall. In a sense we can see the ritual of the masque as a kind of compensation for the scepticism, the predominantly documentary strain that prevailed in the drama of the time— just indeed as the heroic tragedy of the Restoration flourished in a time when men needed the opportunity for escape from political corruption, private disorder and a prudential morality. To the Restoration wit and courtier, Almanzor was a pleasant fancy, a man of principle who believed in such abstractions as love and honour. His admirers did not seriously expect men to be like him, they would have found him embarrassing to meet; but his strong arm and simple faith could provide the basis for a compensating ritual act. To turn back from *The Conquest of Granada* to Heywood's *The Fair Maid of the West* brings out the artificiality of the Restoration heroic style: Heywood, writing for the common people about 1609, writes with the same genuineness as we find in Elizabeth's courtly entertainments; Dryden forces the note like Shirley or Davenant in their masques for Charles and Henrietta.

It is significant that the beginnings of love-and-honour drama are to be found before the Civil War. In the later Fletcher, in Davenant and Shirley we have clear anticipations of the Restoration inflated style and the invoking of abstract principles which provide a basis for unconvincing rhetoric. Vittorio, in Shirley's *The Young Admirall*, acted in 1633, has to choose between his country and his father's life on the one hand and the life of his beloved Cassandra on the other. In the words he speaks there is no conviction, no suggestion that he is other than a theatrical puppet, no hint of the living dilemma that is Macbeth's or Beatrice-Joanna's. Away from its own playhouse such a speech as this can only be ridiculous and bemusing:

> Thunder has struck me;
> I feel new stings about my heart; my father!
> Was ever man so miserably thrown
> Upon despair? if I refuse their war,
> I lose my wife, Cassandra; if I fight,
> My father bleeds. Some divine arm sustain
> My feeble soul, instruct it how I should
> Distinguish sorrow, and which blessing rather
> I should now part with, a dear wife or father.   (III. ii.)

The masques and the foreshadowings of Restoration heroics must be seen then as compensatory exceptions, testifying to the very force of the naturalistic tendency in the drama before the Civil War. They stand aside from the main stream of development, like *Cato* and *Douglas* in the eighteenth century.

Much space has been given here to the attempt to illustrate the change from the predominantly ritual to the predominantly documentary mode, because we need to recognise the especial strength of the tragic style in the earliest years of the seventeenth century. While in *Hamlet* Shakespeare is not yet quite at home in the new fashion and therefore frequently harks back to formalised utterance, the tragedies that follow show complete mastery. In *Lear* above all we find the extraordinary flexibility of this style displayed. There is a formal kind of blank verse, not

with the artificial balances and conceits of early times but
with the weight and dignity of a ceremonial occasion:

> Meantime we shall express our darker purpose.
> Give me the map there. Know that we have divided
> In three our kingdom; and 'tis our fast intent
> To shake all cares and business from our age,
> Conferring them on younger strengths, while we
> Unburden'd crawl toward death. Our son of Cornwall,
> And you, our no less loving son of Albany,
> We have this hour a constant will to publish
> Our daughters' several dowers, that future strife
> May be prevented now. The princes, France and Burgundy,
> Great rivals in our youngest daughter's love,
> Long in our court have made their amorous sojourn,
> And here are to be answer'd. Tell me, my daughters,—
> Since now we will divest us both of rule,
> Interest of territory, cares of state,—
> Which of you shall we say doth love us most?
> That we our largest bounty may extend
> Where nature doth with merit challenge.   Goneril,
> Our eldest-born, speak first.   (I. i.)

Other formalised speeches occur in the rhymed passages
of the first scene, when Kent makes his farewell and France
proclaims his suit for the dowerless Cordelia. But the
rhyme, accentuating the ceremonial touch, takes away
from the speaker the sense of actuality, prevents the too
easy giving of our sympathy to the exiled Kent and the
royal lovers: it is imperative for Shakespeare's purpose
that in this beginning of the play our attention should be
centred in the King and his relations with his daughters.
When we have a passage approaching stichomythia:

> *Lear.*   So young, and so untender?
> *Cordelia.* So young, my lord, and true.   (I. i.)

the employment of broken lines removes the appearance
of a prepared device. In what follows the blank verse

ranges from the relatively formal style of the set speech, as in Lear's first cursing of Goneril, to a free utterance, just perceptibly metrical, as here:

> My wits begin to turn.
> Come on, my boy. How dost, my boy? Art cold?
> I am cold myself. Where is this straw, my fellow?
> The art of our necessities is strange,
> That can make vile things precious. Come, your hovel.
> Poor fool and knave, I have one part in my heart
> That's sorry yet for thee.   (III. ii.)

Prose is used for most of the scenes where Gloucester and Edmund appear together, thus providing us with a kind of stepping-stone to the more remote plane on which Lear's affairs are conducted: the Gloucester-story is not merely parallel with the main plot, emphasising the commonness of the theme: it acts rather in the manner of the old induction, bridging the gap between the audience and a strange tale, yet without the induction's formality which emphasised the gap while striving to bridge it. Lear and his daughters, being tragic figures, have inevitably a vastness of stature, a cosmic significance, that could make them outside the range of our sympathy if they were not closely connected in the play with other characters much nearer to common life. Gloucester, Edmund and Edgar have the function here that Horatio, Rosencrantz and Guildenstern have in *Hamlet*, and the use of prose is one sure way of putting us at our ease with such characters. Prose is used too for Lear in his madness, as indeed was Shakespeare's custom, and we are made more conscious of a mind overthrown through the bringing down of the stately monarch to the level where speech is disordered in form as well as substance. In Act IV Lear is sometimes given a kind of irregular blank verse where the lines are continually broken and where at times the metrical structure altogether collapses: thus we are made to feel the delicate hovering of Lear's wits on the border-line between sanity and insanity, or, as Edgar puts it: "O matter and impertinency mixed; Reason in madness!" Nor in this play is song neglected, providing not a mere lyrical relief but a poignant contrast between the musical form and the ugly disorder of the sequence of events.

Aristotle pointed out that the iambic metre was used for the dialogue portions of Greek tragedies because that metre was nearest to the rhythms of actual speech.[1] Metrical form is required, for tragedy must have that sense of definitive utterance that only metre can give; but only a form close to everyday intercourse will make it possible for the spectator to enter into the presented story and to accept it for the moment as actual. The flexible blank verse of the early seventeenth century, varied with occasional rhyme and prose, fulfilled these requirements better than any other dramatic style that England and perhaps the world have known. In its least formal moments it has exactly the accent of common life, as in Lear's

> O Regan, wilt thou take her by the hand?   (II. iv.)

or in the Duchess of Malfi's

> I pray thee, look thou giv'st my little boy
> Some syrup for his cold, and let the girl
> Say her prayers ere she sleep.   (IV. ii.)

But when it takes on an air of authority and rises to the pitch of formal declamation, it becomes the fitting vehicle for those 'ritual' ideas that still survived: so Ulysses speaks of 'degree' and Edgar of divine justice and Hamlet, albeit in formalised prose, of the splendour of man's position in the great chain of being. Later these notions were to grow weaker, and the later drama therefore had

[1] *The Poetics*, chap. IV.

F

little use for the weightier style, but the condition of tension in early seventeenth-century tragedy made flexibility of utterance essential.

Yet as we read the plays of the great decade we are forced to recognise that this flexible style was the product of inevitable development: it emerged slowly in the last years of the sixteenth century, and first becomes recognisable in Shakespeare's later histories and Marston's *Antonio* plays. The dramatists were not over-conscious of the form of their writing, which was indeed the natural idiom of the theatre of their time. It is very different with nineteenth-century poets writing plays in blank verse: there the straining after an Elizabethan effect makes the playwright self-conscious and shrill. As we saw in Chapter 2, the tragic purposes of the early Jacobean dramatists were not fully apparent to them, so that they blundered strangely when commenting on their plays in prologue and prefatory epistle; so too in the style of their drama they seem to have written in accordance with prevailing custom rather than with the deliberation of a theorist attempting practice. Their results were, of course, far too successful to be the effect of a blind following of fashion: they must have recognised the benefits of the flexible style and the non-formalised utterance, and they could make fun of the early styles of Kyd and Marlowe. But the satisfaction and understanding came after success, and it is doubtful whether they ever fully realised how fitting was the nice balance of formality and informality, reflecting the powerful union of ritual and documentary drama.

Chapter 4

THE TRAGIC EFFECT

WHEN we go to a theatre, we are able to see the action on the stage simultaneously as two separate things. On the one hand, we set ourselves up as judges of the entertainment provided, and comment—at least during the intervals—on the skill of the playing, the effectiveness of the décor, the rightness or wrongness of the producer's interpretation; we even go so far as to comment on the playwright's part, and perhaps single out for praise a skilful piece of writing or planning. To all that extent we are connoisseurs, as in a picture-gallery or antique shop, giving our craftsmen-servants their meed of commendation for having delighted our senses and our judgment. On the other hand, we see the play as something happening in time present, we assume as it were that its development is not determined in advance by the dramatist and his fellow-workers, we grow anxious for the hero's fate, rejoice in his triumph or marvel when we find him still splendid in defeat. Even when we have seen the play before, we still experience a feeling of uncertainty, of hope or fear for the hero's fortunes: it always seems possible that Hamlet will escape the poisoned rapier, that the Witches' promises to Macbeth will not prove treacherous; it is always strangely conceivable that Viola will not win her Duke. It is true that different kinds of drama and different audiences weight the scales one way or the other: a sophisticated spectator, watching a Restoration comedy or—to take an extreme case—a ballet, is not likely to feel greatly perturbed by speculations concerning the outcome of the action; an audience in a provincial nineteenth-century theatre was likely to take its melodrama seriously, to offer advice and warning to the hero, and to hiss the villain even after the play was done. Yet any spectator, watching any kind of play, is to some degree held in suspense and at the same time knows that he is watching a piece of planned make-believe.

It was neglect of this duality of approach that led Samuel Johnson to provide too simple a defence for Shakespeare's disregard of the Unity of Place: no illusion, he said, was broken by a change of scene from Rome to Alexandria because no spectator had ever taken the stage for either.[1] But Samuel Johnson was insensitive to the magic of the theatre, and would find it difficult to believe that a man could feel transported to Elsinore by hearing words spoken by costumed players on a bare stage—and perhaps more securely transported than if he saw a Wagnerian castle rise out of the mists on a cinema screen. Dryden was similarly at fault when he claimed that rhyme gave to dramatic speech the pleasure of a dance-pattern and that, if it is condemned as non-naturalistic, so too is blank verse:[2] he overlooked the fact that, the more obvious the dramatic contrivance, whether in speech or action, the more difficult it is for us to experience illusion: when a certain degree of artificiality is exceeded, our capacity for belief is exhausted.

The actor, too, has his double approach to the drama. He has to 'feel' his part, to get into its 'skin', yet he must remain outside it too, subordinating his share in the play to the total effect which the dramatist has in mind: he must exercise craftsmanship, so that the audience will hear his lines easily and will understand their purport; he must help carry out the producer's general pattern of stage-movement and stage-picture. Mr. John Smith playing

[1] *The Works of Samuel Johnson, LL.D.*, 1796, ii, 96–8.
[2] *Essays of John Dryden*, edited by W. P. Ker, 1926, i. 103.

Othello is neither John Smith nor Othello: he is an actor playing Othello. He must at the same time imagine himself in Othello's situation and know himself outside it. He must pretend, but pretend with all his might and skill. He must not murder Desdemona at every performance, but he must try to convince one part of his own and of each spectator's mind that she actually dies. The point is elementary, but is perhaps worth making because this duality in the mind of the actor is intimately related with the dual vision of the spectator.

In the last chapter it was argued that Elizabethan drama towards the end of the sixteenth century was acquiring a power of illusion greater than it had previously known. Hamlet's words to the players, urging restraint upon them, seem particularly significant here. As the drama was becoming less an affair of ceremonial and more an instrument for representing human life, it was inevitable that modes of acting should be changing too. Hamlet is not merely expressing Shakespeare's impatience, he is recording a development that was in being. When he has counselled the players to let discretion be their tutor and above all to avoid the strutting and bellowing that he has sometimes heard praised, the First Player replies: "I hope we have reformed that indifferently with us." Hamlet's comment on that—"O! reform it altogether"—is an admission that already things are not what they were. It would be rash to attempt descriptions of the acting-styles of Alleyn and Burbage, but we can be in little doubt that Shakespeare's fellows in the first years of the seventeenth century had acquired a degree of restraint that would have puzzled the Alleyn of Marlowe's time. After all, Hamlet found it necessary to warn the players to 'be not too tame neither'. When we add this change in style of acting to the other evidence for an increasing naturalism in early seventeenth-century drama, we can I think assume that the spectator of that time had very much our own dual approach to the plays he saw.

But tragedy has its peculiar antinomies besides those proper to the drama as a whole. As we have seen, the outline of its action seems fore-ordained, whether explicitly through the Witches' prophecies in *Macbeth* or implicitly through the characterisation of Lear and Hamlet and those associated with them. Yet so vigorous do the characters seem, so strongly do they themselves believe in their power of free choice, that as the play proceeds we banish as it were to our subconscious minds the realisation that the end is certain. In Greek tragedy a similar but not identical duality is apparent: there the predetermination of the events is never in doubt, never even half-forgotten, but the characters are free in their thoughts and feelings, they show themselves as worthy of our respect not because of what they do but because of their attitude to the destiny which has been laid down for them. So Electra may be a figure of dignified suffering and resolution in Sophocles, a near-maniac in Euripides, though the pattern of event is the same for both.

Then, too, there is an antithesis in tragedy between the greatness of the hero and his kinship with ourselves. He is, as Aristotle puts it, 'better than we are',[1] a being more fully aware of his situation, more highly organised, more sensitive, than the generality of men, and therefore we look up to him with respect, even if his rashness or ambition leads him to crime, like Oedipus or Macbeth or Vittoria Corombona. Yet he must not be too far removed from us, or we shall fail to see him as humanity's representative and his story will cease to be symbolic of the human situation as a whole. He must have weaknesses and other touches of common humanity. He can be impatient with fools, like Hamlet with Osric; he can express peni-

[1] *The Poetics,* chap. II.

tence for wrong-doing, like Lear with Cordelia; he can be most egregiously deceived, like Othello with Iago; he can indulge in words of affection and gentle railery with those he loves, like the Duchess of Malfi and her husband. Too much of the common touch, and he is too like ourselves, merely one of us and not a symbol of our imagined greatness; too little of it, and he becomes like Dryden's Almanzor, a flight of fancy with whom we can recognise no kinship. Something of greatness, then, and something of common humanity must be in him. But the greatness is balanced also against the certainty of his destruction. We feel pride because so vital a figure stands for humanity; but we feel terror as well because of his inevitable doom. Tragedy simultaneously raises our spirits and shatters them, justifies human life and bids us look to its ultimate vanity.

We have seen, moreover, that the tragic picture of the early seventeenth century involved other oppositions. The orthodox medieval idea of the universe was still powerful: Lear sins against 'degree' by abandoning his kingly power and setting his daughters above his head; Edmund and Macbeth, Claudius and Bussy d'Ambois are destroyed through their ambition, their attempt to usurp a place not theirs according to the natural order; the Duchess of Malfi wantonly disregarded the responsibilities of her rank by marrying beneath her. Yet balanced against this is the view of the world as essentially chaos, in which the sole values are individual ones, in which we feel that Macbeth is more important than his adversaries and the Duchess to be admired for her independence of spirit. So too man is, for Hamlet, a god and a quintessence of dust, kingship is to be striven for yet a man may fish with the worm that hath eat of a king. Both the concept of 'degree' and the Marlowesque aspiration after greatness still exercised authority over the minds of the dramatists, but there was also strong suspicion that cosmos was chaos and man a blind beggar.

Because, however we look at the tragic drama of this time, we find an antinomy, the resultant impression is one of extreme complexity. And we should note that this is stronger in the theatre than in the study, because the dualities in the minds of actor and spectator reinforce the dualities that the text by itself exhibits. Hence, very largely, the fascination of these plays, the impression that we derive from them that we are looking deep into the heart of the human situation. It is not that they present a 'philosophy', as Dante and Milton can be said to do: if we analyse their statements, the component parts stand out as unresolved contradictions. "This shows you are above, ye justicers", says Albany when he knows that Cornwall has died immediately after Gloucester's blinding (IV. ii); yet Lear has cried out: "Is there any cause in nature that makes these hard hearts?" (III. vi). A philosopher would try to reconcile the ideas implicit in these speeches, as he would try to reconcile human free will and divine fore-knowledge, the importance and the wretchedness of man: the dramatist is not concerned with a logical resolution, he is content to express the opposing ideas in close relationship. It is not that he changes his mind, or simply that he makes different characters voice different opinions (as he does for example when Edmund avows man's freedom from planetary influence while his father blames everything on the late eclipses of the sun and moon). The basic contradictions are in the very texture of the plays: in the deaths of the 'guilty' we are made to see that "this even-handed justice Commends the ingredients of our poison'd chalice To our own lips", yet Banquo too is killed.

What we get from these tragedies is therefore not a 'message', any coherent 'explanation' of the condition of humanity, but rather an extraordinarily subtle fusion of points of view. In his earlier years Shakespeare was capable of making us see a dramatic situation from different angles, as when he presented a love-story in *Romeo and Juliet* and made us see it romantically with the lovers themselves and realistically through the eyes of Mercutio and Juliet's Nurse, or as when he gave us the viewpoints of Rosalind and Jaques and made us feel that each was valid. Now in his maturity his plays have come to possess cosmic implications, and the dualities are therefore more numerous and of deeper significance. Our response is towards no particular line of conduct, we are not even led to a preference for some kind of ethical code: rather, we respond to opposing stimuli and are held in a state of tension. The tragedy of Sophocles or Seneca or Thomas Hardy may induce Stoicism, for there the antinomies are more or less logically resolved, but in the Shakespearian tragic picture not even the value of Stoicism is certain. But the degree of this uncertainty is, I think, most clearly brought out by considering two peculiar features of early seventeenth-century tragedy: the co-presence of comedy with the tragedy, and the constant reiteration of the theme of madness.

The tragic drama of this time is of course famous, and has sometimes been considered notorious, for its introduction of comic scenes and characters. This sometimes functions as little more than relief from the tension, as when Hamlet out-euphuises Osric, but often the comic interlude has a deeper significance. The Porter in *Macbeth* and the Fool in *Lear* act as commentators on the action, for the gate to Macbeth's castle has indeed become a kind of hell-gate, and the Fool's facetious remarks on his master's downfall bring it forcibly home to us and slowly to Lear himself. And when the Clown brings the asps to Cleopatra, his simplicity of outlook both heightens the Queen's majesty and hints at its vanity. We are reminded that Cleopatra for all her splendour is of the same species as this honest countryman, and her immortal longings appear somewhat inflated. Shakespeare had indeed done that, with less art, in his earlier writings. Romeo's Apothecary, so much the slave of his poverty that he will break Mantua's law and risk present death, gives a slightly theatrical air to the young hero's resolution to die with Juliet; and even in *The Rape of Lucrece* we have an incident which perhaps Shakespeare had not forgotten when he brought the Clown to Cleopatra: Lucrece summons a groom to carry her message of woe to Collatine; he blushes for very shyness of her presence, and she imagines he is displaying knowledge of her shame. The passage has of course the over-elaborate phrasing of Shakespeare's earliest years, yet the opposition of character presented, the linking of Lucrece and the groom in their common blushing, make her less remote from actuality than she would otherwise appear. It is not comic, in the sense of laughter-provoking, yet it does pull down the tragic figure from her pedestal, it nearly succeeds, where the Clown in *Antony and Cleopatra* succeeds entirely, in making us question the basis of tragic dignity:

> The homely villein curtsies to her low;
> And, blushing on her, with a steadfast eye
> Receives the scroll without or yea or no,
> And forth with bashful innocence doth hie:
> But they whose guilt within their bosoms lie
>> Imagine every eye beholds their blame;
>> For Lucrece thought he blush'd to see her shame:
>
> When, silly groom! Got wot, it was defect
> Of spirit, life, and bold audacity.
> Such harmless creatures have a true respect
> To talk in deeds, while others saucily
> Promise more speed, but do it leisurely:
>> Even so this pattern of the worn-out age
>> Pawn'd honest looks, but laid no words to gage.

His kindled duty kindled their mistrust,
That two red fires in both their faces blaz'd;
She thought he blush'd, as knowing Tarquin's lust,
And, blushing with him, wistly on him gaz'd;
Her earnest eye did make him more amaz'd:
  The more she saw the blood his cheeks replenish,
  The more she thought he spied in her some blemish.

(ll. 1338–58.)

So in *Othello* immediately after the poignant willow-song there is a dialogue in which Emilia's robustness of speech and thought is contrasted with Desdemona's superfine delicacy. The contrast is pointed by Emilia's speaking in prose, Desdemona in blank verse:

Desdemona. Dost thou in conscience think, tell me, Emilia,
That there be women do abuse their husbands
In such gross kind?
  Emilia. There be some such, no question.
  Desdemona. Wouldst thou do such a deed for all the world?
  Emilia. Why, would not you?
  Desdemona. No, by this heavenly light!
  Emilia. Nor I neither by this heavenly light; I might do't
as well i' the dark.
  Desdemona. Wouldst thou do such a deed for all the
    world?
  Emilia. The world is a huge thing; 'tis a great price for a
small vice.
  Desdemona. In troth, I think thou wouldst not.
  Emilia. In troth, I think I should, and undo't when I had
done. Marry, I would not do such a thing for a joint-ring, nor
measures of lawn, nor for gowns, petticoats, nor caps, nor any
petty exhibition; but for the whole world, who would not make
her husband a cuckold to make him a monarch? I should
venture purgatory for't.
  Desdemona. Beshrew me, if I would do such a wrong
For the whole world.
  Emilia. Why, the wrong is but a wrong i' the world; and

75

having the world for your labour, 'tis a wrong in your own world, and you might quickly make it right.

Desdemona. I do not think there is any such woman.

(IV. iii.)

The passage makes us see Desdemona's capacity for self-deception, for Brabantio had kept her in no cloister, and perhaps we begin to wonder too if this woman's conscious virtue is after all so admirable a thing. Does it not depend, we may ask, on a deliberate blindness to the common ways of human nature, and is there not a touch of complacency here—for even Desdemona does not pretend that men are so faithful as she claims women to be?

In these examples from *Antony and Cleopatra* and *Othello* we have seen the comic element influencing our attitude to one of the tragic figures in the play, but the co-presence of comic and tragic in early seventeenth-century drama seems to go even further than this. We have seen that the greatness of the tragic figure is delicately balanced with his kinship with everyday humanity, and that his super-abundant vitality is brought to an ultimate destruction. Because he cannot carve out his own destiny, because he must show recognisable human traits, he is always a potentially comic figure. He must not be too dignified if we are to see him as one of ourselves, yet if we see him for a moment without the protective cloak of dignity, his unavailing struggles in the mesh of circumstance become ludicrous. *The Cherry Orchard* is a comedy, despite its almost unbearable sadness, because the characters have not the clear-sightedness, the poise of tragic figures. But it hovers on the brink of tragedy as one or other of its characters, Madame Ranevsky in particular, seems on the point of acquiring the tragic vision, the defiance of circumstance, the near-arrogance of the tragic hero. *King Lear* is a tragedy, yet throughout there seems to run parallel to the tragic pattern an undercurrent of fierce comedy. If we compare Shakespeare's tragedy either with *Gorboduc* or with the anonymous *Leir* that Shakespeare used as a source-play, we find at once a most striking difference in the handling of the initial situation. Gorboduc, like Lear, divides his kingdom between his children during his own life-time, and all the woe presented in the rest of the play derives from this affronting of 'degree'. But Gorboduc conducts himself always with a stiff dignity: he errs, but with good intent and a sustained solemnity. In the old *Leir* play, the King demands a profession of love from his daughters because he wishes to win the consent of his favourite Cordella to the marriage he has planned for her. But in Shakespeare the King is arrogant and hot-tempered as well as mistaken. The profession of love is demanded merely for his own gratification, the ultimate division of the kingdom is an act of spleen. Moreover, here as elsewhere in the play, Lear is made to apply grotesquely wrong standards: he suggests that the section of the kingdom that he has decreed for each of his daughters will correspond with the degree of her love for him, he will in fact measure love in terms of acres. Later he is to measure it in terms of the number of followers allowed to him: he has cursed Goneril and her unborn child because she would reduce his train from a hundred knights to fifty; when Regan offers to entertain him if he will come with only five-and-twenty knights, he elects to go back to Goneril, saying to her:

> I'll go with thee:
> Thy fifty yet doth double five-and-twenty,
> And thou art twice her love.   (II. iv.)

We are reminded of Hamlet's boast that "forty thousand brothers Could not, with all their quantity of love, Make up my sum" (V. i). In each instance, there is an attempt to apply a numerical estimate of value which is grossly inapplicable. The obtuseness of Lear and Hamlet in these passages is such that their behaviour grows absurd. And when Lear's will is crossed, he assumes a theatrical posture. This is apparent in his exiling of Kent and his repudiation of Cordelia, but it is more degrading when he takes such violent offence at Goneril's quiet words in I. iv and affects not to recognise her. His daughter's self-possession and the Fool's ironical interjections underline the extravagance of the old man's behaviour:

> *Lear.* Does any here know me? This is not Lear:
> Does Lear walk thus? speak thus? Where are his eyes?
> Either his notion weakens, his discernings
> Are lethargied. Ha! waking? 'tis not so.
> Who is it that can tell me who I am?
> *Fool.* Lear's shadow.
> *Lear.* I would learn that; for, by the marks of sovereignty, knowledge and reason, I should be false persuaded I had daughters.
> *Fool.* Which they will make an obedient father.
> *Lear.* Your name, fair gentlewoman? (I. iv.)

Almost immediately comes the terrible cursing of Goneril, which we must see not in relation to Goneril's character as it ultimately displays itself but in relation to what she has so far done: we can then see it as no more justified in its context than Lear's behaviour to Cordelia and Kent in the first scene. The King leaves the scene effectively as soon as the cursing is done: the exit is achieved with authority, but Shakespeare will not let him keep the dignity of his vituperation: almost at once he returns, unpacking his heart with words because he half-realises that words are now the only instruments at his command. He comes back to curse again and to threaten. The authority is gone now, he refers to hot tears on his cheeks and boasts that Regan will be a kinder overlord. And when he finds Regan as obdurate as her sister, we have again his increasingly less precise cursing, his outbreaks of self-pity and posturing, his painful realisation that power has gone from him: there is a dreadful poignancy but an absurdity too in his

> No, you unnatural hags,
> I will have such revenges on you both
> That all the world shall—I will do such things,—
> What they are yet I know not,—but they shall be
> The terrors of the earth. (II. iv.)

It is worth noting that on the modern stage it is almost impossible to play the full text of *Lear* without provoking an embarrassing laughter—when, for example, Lear so persistently clings to his belief in Regan and repeatedly denies the information that Kent gives him:

> *Lear.* What's he that hath so much thy place mistook
> To set thee here?
> *Kent.* It is both he and she,
> Your son and daughter.
> *Lear.* No.
> *Kent.* Yes.
> *Lear.* No, I say.
> *Kent.* I say, yea.
> *Lear.* No, no; they would not.
> *Kent.* Yes, they have.
> *Lear.* By Jupiter, I swear, no.
> *Kent.* By Juno, I swear, ay. (II. iv.)

In the storm-scenes there is less of this, for Lear is beginning to lose his comic self-importance, to grow aware that there are poor naked wretches to whom the pitiless storm is a familiar enemy. Yet even here he can be self-pitying and self-righteous: he can describe himself as a man more sinned against than sinning, and can direct the elements and the gods to visit the guilty with an overdue vengeance. In the madness that then comes upon him he is often grotesque:

79

Arraign her first; 'tis Goneril, I here take my oath before
this honourable assembly, she kicked the poor king her father.
(III. vi.)

He greets the blind Gloucester with "Ha! Goneril, with
a white beard!" and then thinks he sees in Gloucester's
ravaged eye-sockets the inviting glance of a street-walker:

Dost thou squiny at me? No, do thy worst, blind Cupid; I'll
not love. (IV. vi.)

And when the emissaries of Cordelia find him, he runs
from them in a mad frenzy:

Nay, an you get it, you shall get it by running. Sa, sa,
sa, sa. (IV. vi.)

Even at the end of the play, he dies mistaken, believing
that Cordelia still lives: it is deeply moving, but once
again his judgment is at fault, he is brought below the
common level through the magnitude of fortune's last
blow. The wonder is that, despite all this, we recognise
Lear as a tragic hero, a symbol of humanity's greatness in
defeat. But the way in which this is achieved must be considered in a few moments, for it is intimately connected
with Shakespeare's treatment of madness.

If Lear is at times grotesque, absurd, impotent, he is
not alone in that among Shakespeare's tragic heroes.
Hamlet's wild and whirling words, his pathological in-
capacity for the task of revenge, his very extravagance of
jubilation after the play-scene, give to his story too an
undercurrent of grim comedy. And Othello's position as
the husband who is made to think himself a cuckold is
essentially, in Jacobean eyes, ludicrous: the transition
from "My life upon her faith!" (I. iii) to "I have a pain
upon my forehead here" (III. iii) would inevitably amuse
us if the hero's passion were not so great that our smiles
are swallowed up in terror. He is led by the nose as asses

are, and it is not surprising that Thomas Rymer, deter-minedly blind to the probability of the action, found the play merely farcical. Othello feels the same jealousy as Wycherley's Pinchwife, with less justification and more violent results. It is only because of his splendour of language and the grimness of his end that we find the play tragic. But even so there is the same undercurrent of comedy as in *Lear*, the same feeling that, if the focus shifts ever so slightly, we shall laugh.

Mr. T. S. Eliot, speculating on the course that Mar-lowe's genius might have taken if he had lived longer than his twenty-nine years, has suggested that the extravagance of characterisation in Tamburlaine, the Jew of Malta, and the Duke of Guise, indicates that their creator was moving towards the comedy of gigantic caricature that finds its supreme example in *Volpone*.[1] But this judgment may overlook the tragicomic duality that the drama of this time was to achieve. Kyd in *The Spanish Tragedy* was sometimes unconsciously amusing, to his immediate successors as well as to us, but the interpolator who added the Painter's scene gives us that same sense of coexistent tragedy and comedy that we find in *Lear* and *Othello*. And Marlowe, especially in the second part of *Tamburlaine* and in *Edward II*, seems moving towards Jacobean tragedy rather than towards Jonsonian comedy. Jonson was rare indeed in the discipline of his thought, so that vice itself could not take away his faculty for mocking: Marlowe, like Shakespeare and Webster, seems to see things in double focus, so that the play of *Faustus* is simultaneously a morality and a tragedy, and Tamburlaine has the majesty and the gross vanity that we have seen in Lear. Shakespeare's tragic figures have an extravagance of speech and gesture, but the less declamatory style which drama had developed by the early seventeenth century

[1] *Selected Essays*, p. 123.

tends to make it less noticeable than in Marlowe's plays. In all the major tragedies of the great decade there is a frozen laughter which threatens our exaltation at the spectacle of human greatness. The plays thus gain an astringency and a greater power of conviction. We are the readier to accept their picture of life because it confirms our most private judgment, our deepest awareness of universal folly.

Comedy and madness had an association in the Elizabethan mind as they have to-day. We have seen in Lear and Hamlet a touch of the grotesque, not remote from comedy, in the whirling words of Hamlet after the play-scene and by Ophelia's grave and in the frenzy of Lear as he arraigns the absent Goneril and runs crazily from Cordelia's search-party. It is not only the loss of dignity but the loss of awareness, of insight, that brings down the character from the tragic level. Middleton in *The Changeling* makes comedy out of the spectacle of insanity, and before we comment on the insensitivity of the age we should remember many of our own jests on madness and a popular play of recent years that made merry with the theme. Provided that we are sufficiently remote from the afflicted person, madness is indeed material for comedy, for it provides the complete example of a mind and body without conscious control, without the power of comprehending the entangling circumstances. Nevertheless, madness is a constant theme in tragedy, in both Greek and English exemplars. From *The Spanish Tragedy* it is common to find an Elizabethan or Jacobean tragic hero losing mental control, and in Shakespeare's major plays we find Lear actually insane, Hamlet at least on the borderland of madness, Othello falling into a momentary fit; Macbeth too is subject to hallucination, though he never quite loses a sense of the actual: the deepest horror for him is that he knows always the true nature of the evil he does. And

Lady Macbeth has to endure the torment of deranged wits—which is indeed in keeping with her character because, like Hamlet, Othello and Lear, she is from the beginning insufficiently aware of the nature of her acts. In his book *On Hamlet*, Mr. Madariaga has rashly stated that 'mental infirmity is no subject for a tragic author: it belongs to the hospital'.[1] He says this in relation to Hamlet's behaviour at the beginning of the play, before the Ghost has made its revelation, so perhaps he means that, whatever may happen later, a tragic hero should not from the beginning be in a state of mental infirmity. But if so he would seem to overlook two cardinal facts that Shakespeare seems to have been thoroughly familiar with: that there is an extensive borderland between normality and complete insanity, in which the afflicted person may suffer from recurrent or persistent delusions and yet, at the same time, be aware that his mind is diseased; and that certain natures have in them the seeds of madness long before abnormality is easily apparent.

Madness is material for comedy, yet the tragic hero frequently goes mad. Never, however, to the point where, in psychiatric language, 'insight' disappears. The mad creatures of Middleton's *The Changeling* and the crazed figure that runs its course through Jonson's *Bartholomew Fair* live in a world of their own devising: we have little or no contact with them, for neither they nor we can interpret the others' universe. But if, intermittently at least, 'insight' returns, then perhaps the suffering person's comment on our world is made all the keener by the strangeness and horror of his own situation. Hamlet, in his conversation with Polonius after the play-scene, has the embittered aside "They fool me to the top of my bent", after he has rebuked Guildenstern for wishing to play on him as on a recorder (III. ii). Yet in his very impotence

[1] *On Hamlet*, pp. 91–2.

83

of mind he can speak so much to the purpose that Polonius exclaims:

> How pregnant sometimes his replies are! a happiness that often madness hits on, which reason and sanity could not so prosperously be delivered of. (II. ii.)

Lear in his madness comes to see more shrewdly into the ills of the body politic, the hypocrisy and injustice of men, than perhaps any other character in Shakespeare. Schücking has argued that in his denunciation of the administering of human justice we should see only the effect of madness, of a mind disintegrating and failing therefore to find order in the outside world.[1] But that can hardly be the case, not only because Lear's comments have a cogency in their matter and their expression that forces us to recognise them as valid, but because Shakespeare has used Edgar as a chorus-character here to voice his own acceptance of their truth. Lear has spoken of the dog that is obeyed in office, of the rascal beadle who would employ the woman lying beneath his lash, of the usurer whose guilt is as great as the hanged thief's, of the gold that gives vice an impenetrable armour, and then he has relapsed into his raving. Edgar's comment is: "O! matter and impertinency mixed; reason in madness!" (IV. vi). We could not have a clearer hint of how Shakespeare intends us to take Lear's denunciations. It is true that Othello's vision is not clarified when he falls into his fit, but we have already seen that in his play the undercurrent of grim comedy is stronger than elsewhere: Othello has not ever the degree of awareness that the other tragic figures have, and his stature derives solely from the natural eloquence of his speech, the superabundance of his animal vitality.

Thus in all these cases, as in Kyd's Hieronimo, Mar-

---

[1] *Character Problems of Shakespeare's Plays*, 1922, pp. 186–90.

ston's Antonio, Webster's Duchess, we have minds to some extent deranged but still recurrently and indeed generally functioning on the normal plane of experience. So that what they say and do is relevant to our world and can hold our respect. The tragic dramatist is much given to the drawing of mad heroes, because he is aware that the affliction is among the greatest that man can experience, but his heroes must never cross completely into a private world. He will go further with his minor characters, as with Ophelia and Webster's Cornelia, but even with them he will see that their speech has relevance to the general situation and is occasionally a sharp comment on it.

But if the tragedy is to be convincing as a documentation, madness must appear in characters which seem likely to suffer it. This is remarkably the case with Shakespeare, but not for example with Kyd or Marston: we have no justification for the frenzies of Hieronimo or of Antonio in *Antonio and Mellida*. We should not, of course, implant in Shakespeare psychological notions that were unknown in his day, but there is no need to do that in order to demonstrate that Hamlet, Ophelia, Lady Macbeth, Lear and Othello were likely victims. Because Shakespeare was a supreme observer of human nature, it is not surprising that he saw the germ of possible madness in Hamlet's veneration for his father and persistent dwelling on his mother's sexuality, in Ophelia's secretiveness and rigid restraint of manner, in Lady Macbeth's deliberate blinding of herself to the nature of her crime, in Lear's morbid egotism and assertiveness and possessiveness, and in Othello's blind trust and strange lack of self-knowledge. Because in each of these cases the mental derangement is in accord with the character, the play gains markedly in its power of conviction. As a document of human life it rings true. The fit of insanity is no *diabolus ex machina*, no wanton turning of the screw. Rather, it strengthens our

85

impression that in these tragedies we are looking deep into the human condition.

But so it is, and more subtly, with the mad speeches and actions. We have the experience that we share the world-out-of-focus that Lear, for example, inhabits. We have contact with him because of his continuing 'insight', and therefore it is that we have here an extreme example of the multiplicity of viewpoint that we have found character-istic of Shakespearian drama. When Lear is voicing his fierce criticism of the world as we know it, we come al-most to doubt the ultimate value of sanity itself. That doubt is much stronger in *Troilus and Cressida* and *Timon of Athens*, but even in the four great tragedies we have only the most fleeting hold on values. The general im-pression we derive from these plays is that humanity can justify itself through its power to suffer and to compre-hend its suffering, but even of that Shakespeare does not leave us entirely sure. At the end of things, in the ultimate sad analysis, we are not sure what 'greatness' is, we are pitifully aware that our capacity to suffer has a breaking-point, that our powers of comprehension are dim. Rem-nants of old faiths jut out now and then like rocks in a troubled sea, but there is no firm footing on them, and the sea is limitless, the laws of its tides unknown, its winds incalculable. The castaway swims vigorously, scans the encompassing horizon.

Chapter 5

RYMER ON "OTHELLO"

IT is easy to make fun of Thomas Rymer. He was a learned, pugnacious and foolhardy man who gave the quasi-immortality of publication to critical judgments that he knew could not be popular. In his short book *The Tragedies of the Last Age, Consider'd and Examin'd By the Practice of the Ancients, and By the Common Sense of all Ages*, which first appeared in 1678, he set out to decry the Elizabethan dramatic legacy to the Restoration. There is no attack on Webster or Ford or Marlowe here, for their plays found little or no place in the theatre of Rymer's age: instead he singled out Fletcher and Shakespeare for his attack, and rated even Jonson as an insufficiently regular poet. He knew that *Othello* and *The Maid's Tragedy* and *A King and No King* would remain theatrical favourites in his day; he recognised that these plays gave opportunities for impressive acting; yet he stood out and lashed them with the strength of his whole arm. His book began with the statement that he would deal with three plays associated with the names of Beaumont and Fletcher (*Rollo, The Maid's Tragedy* and *A King and No King*), two by Shakespeare (*Othello* and *Julius Caesar*), and one by Jonson (*Catiline*), but he found that his volume was full when he had given his views on the Fletcher plays and so postponed for a time his consideration of Shakespeare and Jonson. It was not until 1692 that the sequel appeared, with the impressive title, *A Short View of Tragedy; It's Original, Excellency, and Corruption. With some Reflections on Shakespeare, and other Practitioners for the Stage*. This is an attempt to consider tragedy both historically and theoretically. Rymer traces its development from Athens through medieval and Renaissance Europe,—until he lights on the play of *Othello* and pours out his venom. Briefer and less harsh words on *Julius Caesar* and *Catiline* conclude his labours.

To-day he is largely known for the grossest absurdities that can be found in the pages of these two books. *Othello* in its 'tragical part', he says, is 'plainly none other, than a Bloody Farce, without salt or savour'.[1] Shakespeare's powers of expression win the admiration of play-goers, he tells us, but "In the *Neighing* of an Horse, or in the *growling* of a Mastiff, there is a meaning, there is as lively expression, and, may I say, more humanity, than many times in the tragical flights of *Shakespeare*."[2] Iago, he is sure, is a badly drawn character: soldiers have everywhere the reputation of being 'open-hearted, frank, plain-dealing'; Iago is a soldier; therefore Iago ought to be 'open-hearted, frank, plain-dealing' and Shakespeare was wrong to present him otherwise.[3] Evadne in *The Maid's Tragedy* is a woman, and therefore should be modest, as is the nature of women: Beaumont and Fletcher, in showing her unchaste and foul-mouthed, sinned against the common knowledge of the female character.[4] Rymer, of course, was not so foolish as to believe that all women were modest, all soldiers 'open-hearted, frank, plain-dealing', but he had read in Aristotle that poetry presents a general truth, not the particular truth of history:[5] he believed, therefore, that a poet must always present a generalisation, the accepted idea of a type of character, and he was naïve enough to think that women and soldiers generally bore high reputations. Even so, he did not reason sharply enough to see that the categories

---

[1] *A Short View of Tragedy*, 1693, p. 146. [2] *Ibid.*, pp. 95–6.
[3] *Ibid.*, pp. 93–4. [4] *The Tragedies of the Last Age*, 1692, p. 113.
[5] *The Poetics*, chap. IX.

'women' and 'soldiers' were different, though in his day of more or less exclusively professional soldiering it was easier than it would be now to think of a soldier as a special variety of the human species.

He is often led astray, too, by his belief that the drama should reflect social decorum. In *The Maid's Tragedy* he is shocked because Evadne kills the King, whose willing mistress she has been. This must be wrong, for it is both regicide and an unwarrantably feminist act. "If I mistake not," says Rymer,

> in Poetry no woman is to kill a man, except her quality gives her the advantage above him, nor is a Servant to kill the Master, nor a Private Man, much less a Subject to kill a King, nor on the contrary. Poetical decency will not suffer death to be dealt to each other by such persons, whom the Laws of Duel allow not to enter the lists together.[1]

We are forced to stay for a moment to consider how sweeping is this last assertion: Orestes' killing of Clytemnestra, Medea's of her children, the killing of Cornwall in *King Lear* by the brave servant who tried to save Gloucester from blindness, and of course the deaths of Vittoria Corombona and the Duchess of Malfi, with some hundreds of other Elizabethan slaughters—not only are these morally reprehensible, which is arguable, but they should never be incorporated into a tragic action. After this we may understand that Rymer's view of tragedy inevitably led him into wholesale denunciation. Many of us have tried to define tragedy and have found ourselves forced by our definition to exclude from the kind many plays commonly regarded as tragic—Dr. I. A. Richards, for example, labels as 'pseudo-tragedy' nearly all the Elizabethan claimants except half a dozen of Shakespeare's [2]—

[1] *The Tragedies of the Last Age*, p. 117.
[2] *Principles of Literary Criticism*, p. 247.

but Rymer, if he had pushed his enquiries to their limit, might well have been left with no tragedies at all.

But he is patriotic, and for his country's sake will stretch decorum a little:

> There may be circumstances that alter the case, as when there is a sufficient ground of partiality in an *Audience*, either upon the account of *Religion* (as *Rinaldo*, or *Riccardo* in *Tasso* might kill *Soliman*, or any other *Turkish* King or great *Sultan*) or else in favour of our *Country* for then a private *English Heroe* might overcome a King of some Rival Nation.[1]

So that if Macbeth had only been an Englishman, if Tamburlaine a Christian, their treatment of Duncan and Bajazet might have passed muster.

Rymer, however, was not content with theory. *The Tragedies of the Last Age* was licensed by Sir Roger L'Estrange on July 17, 1677: on September 13 of the same year he gave his sanction to *Edgar, or The English Monarch; An Heroick Tragedy By Thomas Rymer of Grays-Inn Esq.*, a play that never reached the stage but was reprinted in 1691 and 1693 and was remembered for some time as an imprudent exhibition of a critic's limitations in the practical field. Addison, writing in *The Spectator* on September 10, 1714—twenty-seven years after *Edgar*'s first appearance—referred to some recent progress in stage-contrivances. The playhouses, he said,

> are also provided with above a dozen showers of snow, which, as I am informed, are the plays of many unsuccessful poets artificially cut and shredded for that use. Mr. Rymer's Edgar is to fall in snow at the next acting of King Lear, in order to heighten, or rather to alleviate, the distress of that unfortunate prince; and to serve by way of decoration to a piece which that great critic has written against.

Of course, Addison's memory had tricked him. We might dearly love to have Rymer's critique of *Lear*, but we must

---

[1] *The Tragedies of the Last Age*, pp. 117–18.

be content with his animadversions on *Othello* and *Julius Caesar*. It is clear, however, that the game of making fun with Rymer was well and truly begun by 1714. And while the history of literary criticism remains a subject of university study, the game is likely to go on.

Edgar, or The English Monarch, written in the fashionable rhyming couplets, is beyond question a very bad play. It aims at embodying in its hero the greatness of the English monarchy, and shows kings from foreign countries paying homage to Edgar and, remarkably, acknowledging his supremacy over the seas. In the prefatory Advertisement, Rymer defends the happy ending of his *Heroick Tragedy* by invoking the name of Euripides, and, in a note after the list of dramatis personae, he proudly draws our attention to the fact that "The time of the Representation" extends "from Twelve at Noon to Ten at Night"—a triumph of dramatic regularity that doubtless qualified him for the scourging of Shakespeare's wanton change of scene from Venice to Cyprus in *Othello*.[1] We might indeed expect dullness in *Edgar*, but we get instead a welter of incommunicable passion. Edgar is just married to Ethelwold's daughter, but sees and immediately loves Ethelwold's newly-married and as yet virgin wife: he struggles with his desires, as does the lady with hers, but they are made free to marry when Ethelwold kills Edgar's wife, thinking it is his own wife who is waiting for Edgar in the dark. In the last scene Dunstan, the Archbishop of Canterbury, tells Edgar he still cannot marry his beloved, because he has been a godfather to her and the Pope will not allow this spiritual relationship to be overlooked: Edgar thereupon shows an Anglican independence of mind and will have no such Papal interference. It is all unbelievably stilted in manner and unhistorical in feeling. If only the play were a little livelier,

---

[1] *A Short View of Tragedy*, p. 106.

it would be ridiculous. As it is, the love-tangles pall and Rymer strains our charity.

It says much for Rymer's powers of persuasion that he was respected as a critic in spite of *Edgar* and in spite of his ruthless attacks on Shakespeare and Fletcher. G. K. Chesterton, describing how the young Bernard Shaw came to England and determined to be recognised as a revolutionary, bids us imagine his hero trying to find something to denigrate which all other men revered: religion and government were, after all, everyday targets for abuse, and no young man, even in late Victorian England, would win much attention by attacking them, but there was one object of universal reverence, one theme for praise by tory and radical, by evangelical and freethinker, one sure means of gaining the revolutionary label. The young Shaw, in fact, rocked the world of polite culture by showing a wholesome irreverence in his remarks on Shakespeare.[1] It was not quite the same in Restoration days, but we must remind ourselves of the already entrenched position which Shakespeare had won in the theatre by 1680: his plays were securely in the repertory, he had been praised by Jonson, the one Elizabethan rival who could be used to exhibit his irregularity, and he had won the continuing and enthusiastic, though sometimes qualified, esteem of Dryden, the man who bestrides the little world of Restoration literature as its recognised Colossus.

Yet Rymer won sometimes praise and always respect. One of Dryden's most ambitious pieces of dramatic theorising, the *Preface to Troilus and Cressida*, was published in 1679, shortly after the appearance of *The Tragedies of the Last Age*: there Dryden writes clearly under Rymer's influence, rejecting the unclassical barbarism of tragicomedy, which elsewhere he defended, and

[1] *George Bernard Shaw*, 1926, pp. 101–2.

showing in his adaptation of Shakespeare's play that he has fully accepted Rymer's notion of tragic drama: without apparent irony he refers his readers to Rymer's work and alludes to him as 'our English critic'.[1] John Dennis, writing his lively series of dialogues, *The Impartial Critick*, in 1693, the year of *A Short View of Tragedy*, expressed his disagreement with Rymer's view of Shakespeare, but merely urged that Waller, who was Rymer's poetic idol, would also reveal faults if subjected to the close analytic method which Rymer had used for *Othello*. Like most other critics of the Restoration and early eighteenth century, Dennis admits that Shakespeare has plenty of faults, but pleads that his good qualities atone for them.[2] In Spence's *Anecdotes* we read Pope's opinion:

> Rymer a learned and strict critic? Ay, that is exactly his character. He is generally right, though rather too severe in his opinion of the particular plays he speaks of; and is, on the whole, one of the best critics we ever had.[3]

As Spingarn pointed out, this is a far cry from Macaulay's characteristic assertion that Rymer was 'the worst critic that ever lived':[4] it suggests, too, that the man whose

---

[1] *Essays of John Dryden*, edited by W. P. Ker, i. 212. Later, however, Dryden seems to have wearied of Rymer's attitude: in the Dedication to *Examen Poeticum* (1693), he shows impatience at Rymer's condescending advice in *A Short View of Tragedy*, and it is surely to Rymer that these couplets refer in the prologue to *Love Triumphant* (1694), where the poet bids farewell to the stage:

> To Shakespear's Critique, he bequeaths the Curse,
> To find his faults; and yet himself make worse.
> A precious Reader in Poetique Schools,
> Who by his own Examples damns his Rules.

Cf. Dryden. *The Dramatic Works*, edited by Montague Summers, 1931–2, vi. 580–1.

[2] *Critical Essays of the Seventeenth Century*, edited by J. E. Spingarn, 1909, iii. 197.

[3] *Ibid.*, i. lxxix.   [4] *Ibid., loc. cit.*

standing was so high with Dryden and Pope, despite *Edgar*, despite his judgments on Iago and Evadne, was no mere target for a lecturer's raillery. In recent years, indeed, Mr. T. S. Eliot has more than once put in a semi-surreptitious good word for him. There is a footnote in Mr. Eliot's essay on *Hamlet*, published in 1919, which tells us: "I have never, by the way, seen a cogent refutation of Thomas Rymer's objections to *Othello*." [1] And in another footnote, to the essay on *Four Elizabethan Dramatists* published in 1924, we read that "Rymer makes out a very good case". [2]

I am scarcely trying in this chapter to offer a 'cogent refutation'. Rather, I am seeking an explanation of Rymer's attitude to the play of *Othello*, principally because it may lead to some further study of the nature of tragedy, and particularly of that kind of tragedy which flourished in England from the beginning of the seventeenth century to the closing of the theatres. And we may be able to see not only why that tragedy so repelled Thomas Rymer but why it is that in our day Thomas Eliot too approaches the Jacobeans with deep interest and grave discomfort.

We will do well, as a beginning, to note that not a little in *The Tragedies of the Last Age* and *A Short View of Tragedy* is acutely judged and wittily phrased. In his account of *A King and No King* Rymer is offended, as most of us are to-day, by the sudden turn of events in the last act: the supposed King has fallen in love with his supposed sister, and for four acts the play hovers giddily over the incest-theme; then Act V brings a bundle of revelations, the King is no king, his supposed sister is the real Queen, they are free to marry and do so. Rymer questions why we are given no previous hint of the line which the plot ultimately takes, why in the name of probability the characters that knew the secret remained so

[1] *Selected Essays*, p. 141.　　　[2] *Ibid.*, p. 116.

obstinately silent, and why Beaumont and Fletcher gave
to such a play so lighthearted-sounding a title.[1] When he
turns to *The Maid's Tragedy*, he points out that Aspatia,
the 'maid' of the title, is not one of the chief characters
and therefore should not give the play its name.[2] Moreover, the King, who wished to marry his mistress Evadne
to a husband who would be conveniently complacent,
would not have chosen the honest and valiant Amintor as
his victim.[3] Rymer sees too that the presentation of the
injured Aspatia is unconvincing to a sober eye, that here
Beaumont and Fletcher engineer a pathetic situation
merely for the sake of its theatrical effectiveness.[4] When
the wronged Amintor reveals Evadne's guilt to her
brother Melantius, they draw swords in turn and each in
turn finds it impossible to defend himself against his
friend: on the printed page the scene is as ridiculous as
Rymer claims, and he shrewdly points out that it is
successful on the Restoration stage only because the actors
Hart and Mohun hold the spectators with the magic of
voice and gesture.[5] Rymer is perhaps a little over-
reluctant to admit Fletcher's skill in writing scenes for
accomplished actors to exercise their craft in, but such
intellectual puritanism is a fault in a relatively blameless
direction.

In writing on Beaumont and Fletcher, Rymer has
indeed given us critical points which are now common
currency. That is not the case with his judgment of
Othello, yet even there the reader can appreciate the
critic's rough wit. After summarising the plot, he thus
delivers himself:

> What ever rubs or difficulty may stick on the Bark, the Moral,
> sure, of this Fable is very instructive.

---

[1] *The Tragedies of the Last Age*, p. 57.
[2] *Ibid.*, p. 105.
[3] *Ibid.*, pp. 107–9.
[4] *Ibid.*, pp. 123–5.
[5] *Ibid.*, pp. 133–9.

1. First, This may be a caution to all Maidens of Quality how, without their Parents consent, they run away with Blackamoors. . . .

Secondly, This may be a warning to all good Wives, that they look well to their Linnen.

Thirdly, This may be a lesson to Husbands, that before their Jealousie be Tragical, the proofe may be Mathematical.[1]

Now, if we look for a 'moral' in *Othello*, I think we shall come to the conclusion that Rymer has accurately though irreverently given it to us. His denunciation of the play is based on a false premiss: granted that premiss, granted that we should find in all tragic plays a support for current morality, we can hardly defend Shakespeare. But we must postpone for a few moments a consideration of Rymer's basic assumptions.

His close study of the play led him to see that the time-scheme is self-contradictory. In I. iii, immediately before sailing for Cyprus, Roderigo goes to sell all his land, yet on his second day in the island he tells Iago: "My money is almost spent" (II. iii). Rymer's comment is: "The Venetian squire had a good riddance for his Acres. The Poet allows him just time to be once drunk, a very conscionable reckoning!"[2] On the same day Iago puts thoughts of jealousy into Othello's mind: he insinuates, and makes Othello believe, that Desdemona has been unfaithful, and habitually so: yet there was literally no time for this to happen, if we except the short morning-interview of Desdemona and Cassio which Othello's arrival interrupted.[3] Then it is seemingly yet the same day when, in III. iv, Bianca reproaches Cassio for having absented himself a whole week: he had only been two days on the island, and so diligent a reader as Rymer is forced to the conclusion either that the poet was un-

---

[1] *A Short View of Tragedy*, p. 89. [2] *Ibid.*, p. 116.
[3] *Ibid.*, pp. 121-3.

conscionably careless or that Bianca's hot affections had played a singular trick with her memory.[1] Of course, later critics have seen these difficulties in the text, and Bradley expressed dissatisfaction with Christopher North's ingenious theory of 'long-time' and 'short-time', which argued that Shakespeare needed a period of some length within which the action and alleged action of the play might be possible, but that he also wanted to give an impression of rapid, unhalting movement towards the catastrophe: consequently he gave two series of time-references, which are not consistent with one another but do not appear to clash in the theatre.[2] The theory may indeed suggest too much deliberation on Shakespeare's part, and perhaps we are more likely to see in the time-references in *Othello* an illustration of what Schücking has called 'episodic intensification'. Despite the constant fluidity of the action in Elizabethan drama, the dramatists aimed at producing the maximum effect from each single scene: thus in *The Tempest*, V. i, Prospero claims that

> graves at my command
> Have wak'd their sleepers, op'd, and let them forth
> By my so potent art.

though we know that there have been no risings from the dead on the enchanted island.[3] So here in *Othello* Shakespeare did not consider collating his time-references: in each scene he used whichever seemed most appropriate to his immediate purpose. But all this is the fruit of the most illuminated Shakespearian scholarship, and we cannot be surprised that Rymer, reading the play with unusual care, could not justify its apparent incoherence. Shakespeare,

---

[1] *Ibid.*, p. 127.   [2] *Shakespearean Tragedy*, 1905, pp. 423–9.
[3] *Character Problems in Shakespeare's Plays*, pp. 113–19. But for further comment on this passage from *The Tempest*, cf. below, p. 143.

formerly an actor and still a house-keeper, aimed at and achieved a unity of impression in the theatre: it would not have occurred to him that minor contradictions, unnoticeable in the theatre, had any importance whatever.

We shift our ground a little when we consider certain moments in the play where Rymer was not sufficiently sensitive to appreciate the subtlety of Shakespeare's craft. In I. iii, after Brabantio has abandoned his claim to Desdemona, the Duke of Venice offers him consolation in sententious couplets, to which Brabantio replies in the same style. Rymer finds this capping of sentences as absurd as anything in *The Rehearsal*,[1] and it may well appear so to a reader who has not observed it as a common device in Shakespeare and has not therefore speculated on its dramatic function. We may compare these speeches of Brabantio and the Duke with the farewell speech of Kent and the last exchanges of Lear and the King of France in the first scene of *King Lear*. In a serious part of the dramatic action, the function of rhyme is to lower the tension: it fantasticates the play, removes it farther from the spectators' orbit, and consequently diminishes their concern: the rhymed sententiousness of the Duke and Brabantio, by affording an interval of rest, allows for the transition from Othello's winning of Desdemona to the plans for battle with the Turk. Rymer is similarly shocked by the witty exchanges between Desdemona and Iago in II. i, while they are awaiting Othello's arrival: it seems to Rymer most inappropriate that, in a time of war and when the very life of the Venetian general is in doubt, the general's wife should cultivate a light-hearted air.[2] He overlooks the fact that Shakespeare underlines Desdemona's anxiety and uses the gallant comedy she plays as a means of increasing our knowledge of her secretiveness: the woman who says here, aside:

---

[1] *A Short View of Tragedy*, pp. 103–5.   [2] *Ibid.*, pp. 110–12.

I am not merry, but I do beguile
The thing I am by seeming otherwise.

is indeed the daughter whose elopement had left her
father guessing, who was to prevaricate when Othello
demanded the handkerchief, and who finally and pathetic-
ally tried to take on herself the responsibility for her own
death. In the same scene, Rymer objects to the rhetorical
welcome given to Desdemona by Cassio when she lands
from her ship:

O! behold,
The riches of the ship is come on shore.
Ye men of Cyprus, let her have your knees.
Hail to thee, lady! and the grace of heaven,
Before, behind thee, and on every hand,
Enwheel thee round!

Rymer's comment is: "In the name of phrenzy, what
means this Souldier? or would he talk thus, if he meant
any thing at all?" [1] Indeed the situation looks over-written
on paper, but Rymer does not see the symbolism of effect
here: Desdemona, arriving on the island where she is to
be humiliated and done to death, becomes the centre of
homage, is allowed to know the peak of her fortune. We
must remember that, in *Othello* as in all the great tragedies,
there are throughout presages of disaster: we know already
that ill is to befall Desdemona and Othello, and it is therefore tragically ironic that Desdemona's arrival should be
so splendid. Its rhetoric, moreover, is appropriate enough
to the Elizabethan stage.

In all these matters we can think Rymer mistaken but
pardonably so. It is different when we turn to his objections which are based on a failure to appreciate the full
range of possibilities in human action. He is horrified by
Desdemona's marriage to Othello, because of the difference in colour: because he is horrified, he escapes into

[1] *Ibid.*, p. 110.

incredulity. It might have been well enough, he argues, if Desdemona had had a blackamoor nurse from whom she had sucked a vagrancy of the blood, but he cannot believe that a true senator's daughter would embark on a course of action that was not to the taste of a scholarly Englishman of the Restoration.[1] Moreover, he cannot credit that the Venetian senate would tolerate the marriage: certainly, he says, our own House of Lords would have taken a sterner view.[2] This is to be related to his belief that Evadne in *The Maid's Tragedy* would not have behaved to Amintor as she did on their wedding-night,[3] that Panthea in *A King and No King* would not have submissively accepted Arbaces as her husband after he had behaved so outrageously.[4] So, too, he cannot understand that Iago should include Desdemona among his victims: against Cassio and Othello he had grounds for malice, but not against her.[5] The answer is, of course, that such things as these are indeed common: love is not infrequently given to the stranger, and the colour of his skin is of no more importance than his degree of intelligence or his character; senators are notoriously unconcerned with private issues; a proud woman not kindred of her bridegroom's soul may behave with the ferocity of Evadne to Amintor; many a woman will forgive a good deal of violent conduct, if it is occasioned by love of her; and a mind poisoned with conceit of itself, as Iago's is, does not look for guilt in its choice of victims.

Rymer is shocked too by the grossness of much of the language in *Othello*. Many of to-day's readers seem to overlook this, perhaps through an insufficient acquaintance with Elizabethan English, but certainly there is a heavy sensuality in this play's language which marks it out

---

[1] *A Short View of Tragedy*, p. 151.   [2] *Ibid.*, p. 102.
[3] *The Tragedies of the Last Age*, pp. 111–13.   [4] *Ibid.*, pp. 67–8.
[5] *A Short View of Tragedy*, pp. 126–7.

among Shakespeare's major tragedies. In *Hamlet* there is broad railing, in *Lear* a fierce expression of revulsion from sexuality, but here the atmosphere is sultry and fully charged with images of desire. It is not for nothing that Cassio's drunkenness interrupts Othello's wedding-night, that Iago's thoughts in soliloquy flit round the prone form of Desdemona, that he speculates on the possibility of unfaithfulness in her, and more than once suspects that Othello has had Emilia for his mistress—not for nothing that, by Iago's contrivance, Othello rouses Desdemona from sleep in order to kill her. To find another play so heavily charged with sexual passion, we should have to look forward twenty-five years to Ford's *'Tis Pity She's a Whore*. Rymer, however, is hardly conscious of all this. His horror at Desdemona's marriage may be partly due to some awareness of the play's atmosphere, but his objection is explicit only with reference to Iago's language to Brabantio in I. i and to Othello's treatment of Desdemona in IV. ii, where he pretends to see her as a woman for sale.[1] Certainly the first scene is worthy of study for the violence of image with which Iago assaults Brabantio's ear. We must remember that Iago had no grudge against the senator: he was gross for his own sake, because his own mind could not free itself from the images that he gave words to. We may owe Rymer a debt if he makes us aware of this characteristic of the play.

If we want a clear illustration of what Rymer believed true tragedy ought to be, we should turn to the first chapter of *A Short View of Tragedy*. There he outlines the sequence of events in an unwritten play, *The Invincible Armado*, closely modelled on the *Persians* of Aeschylus. When he wrote *Edgar*, Rymer was trying to minister to public taste as well as to write correctly, but here he is the pure theoriser, accompanying his precepts with a brief

[1] *Ibid.*, pp. 96–8, 130.

illustration of how they can be put into practice. The place
of action was to be '*at* Madrid, *by some* Tomb, *or solemn
place of resort*', the time 'Twelve at Night'. The first act
shows a number of grandees of Spain, who, resolving
themselves into the Chorus, descant on their country's
greatness. In the second act news is brought that it was to
conquer England that the Armada had set sail, and the
Chorus rejoices in the certainty of success and the magnitude of the conquest. The third act shows quarrelling
among the nobility as to the sharing of the yet unwon
booty. The fourth reveals that 'old Dames of the Court'
have had dreams and premonitions of disaster, and the
last brings messengers to the King, who learns and
bewails his defeat. This outline Rymer recommends to
Dryden.[1] Now, whatever one may think of *The Invincible
Armado*, it is not ridiculous as *Edgar* is. It could even be
'tragic' in the sense in which we understand the word,
illustrating the irony of hope, the bitterness of defeat, the
gradual coming of a solemn awareness that life is a thing
to be endured. But Rymer does not see it like that at all:
for him it has much the same function as a military tattoo
—to arouse patriotic sentiment and ancestor-worship. For
him the stage should be 'our school of good manners',[2]
the end of tragedy 'to shew *Virtue in Triumph*':[3] poetic
justice must be carefully dispensed, so that the guilty are
always punished and they who suffer are never innocent.
Rymer was not so blind as to think that such justice was
to be found in actuality, but he puts forward an ingenious
argument in maintaining that it must be found in poetry.
Because 'the *unequal* distribution of rewards and punishments did perplex the *wisest*', the Greeks concluded

> that a *Poet* must of necessity see *justice* exactly administred, if
> he intended to please. For, said they, if the World can scarce

---

[1] *A Short View of Tragedy*, pp. 13–17.
[2] *Ibid.*, pp. 99–100.   [3] *Ibid.*, p. 49.

be satisfi'd with God Almighty, whose holy will and purposes are not to be *comprehended*; a *Poet* (in these matters) shall never be pardon'd, who (they are sure) is not *incomprehensible*; whose *ways* and *walks* may, without *impiety*, be penetrated and examin'd.[1]

That is, a poet is not concerned with presenting life as it is, but is to simplify and rectify; it is not his province to question the ways of God; rather, assuming the goodness of the divine plan, he is to write in such a way as to increase the general respect for inherited law. Tragedy may end fortunately, as for Edgar of England, or unfortunately, as for Philip of Spain, but in each case justice must be done. In view of this, *Othello* is especially repugnant to him: towards the end of his examination of the play, he writes:

> Rather may we ask here what unnatural crime *Desdemona*, or her Parents had committed, to bring this Judgment down upon her; to Wed a Black-amoor, and innocent to be thus cruelly murder'd by him. What instruction can we make out of this Catastrophe? Or whither must our reflection lead us? Is not this to envenome and sour our spirits, to make us repine and grumble at Providence; and the government of the World? If this be our end, what boots it to be Vertuous?[2]

This indeed is the heart of his criticism, rather than his better known but merely abusive description of the play as a 'Bloody Farce'. "If this be our end, what boots it to be Vertuous?" Rymer realised far more clearly than most critics that *Othello* and Shakespeare's other great tragedies present a view of the world that cannot be reconciled with Christianity.

That indeed, as we saw in Chapter 1, is true of Elizabethan tragedy generally. Marlowe's heroes are fiery meteors who blaze defiantly and are quenched: though, like most Elizabethans, Marlowe does not remain con-

[1] *The Tragedies of the Last Age,* p. 14.
[2] *A Short View of Tragedy,* pp. 141, 138 (consecutive pages).

sistent throughout a single play, the strongest feeling that characterises his drama is one of sympathy with the man who dares to challenge Fate: his guilt is hardly greater than other men's, and he is to be admired for the scope of his ambition and for his freedom from common hesitation. In Webster's *The White Devil*, moreover, there is admiration for the pattern of ruthlessness offered by Vittoria and Flamineo to a corrupt world: in their awareness of the immanence of evil, in their freedom from fear, these characters have a splendour about them denied to the comparatively guiltless Cardinal. In the person of the Duchess of Malfi Webster shows us dignity and simple goodness allied to resolution, and the violence of her fate is the more terrible for its injustice: the world of this play is one where mercy is withheld from men, where a guiltless woman can be tortured to death, and where her brother the murderer cannot be cruel to her without tearing at his own heart-strings. Similarly in all other early seventeenth-century tragic plays—in Chapman's and Ford's, for example—there is a picture of a world in which there is no necessary relation between deserts and rewards, in which the gods seem indifferent to suffering, and in which men and women are frequently valued by the dramatist for their daring and pride of spirit—qualities that may well bring them into conflict with traditional morality. Historians of the drama often speak of Webster and Ford as belonging to the 'decadence', but that judgment largely depends on an imperfect appreciation of Marlowe and Chapman and Shakespeare. Shakespeare as much as Ford saw his characters as led to their doom, not because they deserved it but because their characters and situations were such that doom was inescapable. Professor Allardyce Nicoll has stressed that the streak of naïveté in Othello, the secretiveness which was second nature to Desdemona, were contributory factors in the tragic development of the story.¹ Neither of them deserves his end, but that end arises naturally and necessarily from all that precedes. Moreover, these characters are caught up in the toils of their own strong passions: we admire them for the very vehemence with which they suffer, but we are simultaneously repelled by the extravagance of their subjection. It is perhaps not out of place to compare Othello, Desdemona and Iago with the men and women in M. Jean-Paul Sartre's novel, *L'Âge de Raison*: alike they are the slaves of passion, but Shakespeare's figures emerge as tragic because they contrive to believe in themselves, they cling hard to a stoical self-respect. This stoicism, derived from antiquity and especially from Seneca, is the individual's sole remaining defence in a world whose purpose cannot be fathomed. It is an essentially pagan attitude and from the Christian viewpoint is neither necessary nor helpful in the human situation. Not infrequently it breaks down, as in *Timon of Athens* and the plays of Cyril Tourneur, where we have something approaching pure nihilism or an uneasy mingling of that with orthodox belief. It is therefore not surprising that Rymer and Mr. Eliot are equally in their different ways abashed by the view of human life afforded by Jacobean tragedy. Rymer sees *Othello* as leading man from the path of virtue, Eliot finds its attitude to life inadequate, a mere attempt to cheer oneself up in a situation that logically should breed either faith or despair.

If we turn from Jacobean tragedy to the serious drama of the Restoration, the gulf between the two seems hardly to be bridged. In the heroic dramas of Dryden and Lee, in the pathetic plays of Otway and Southerne, there is everywhere decorum.² The Restoration period, notorious

---

¹ *Studies in Shakespeare*, 1927, pp. 89–91, 104–8.

² The scenes of comic relief in Otway and Southerne belong to a different world from that of the main actions of the plays.

for its frankness of speech and amorality of outlook in comedy, is in tragedy as conventionally minded as Victorian melodrama. Love and honour may struggle for mastery in Almanzor's breast, but he will be conscious of his heroic position and will keep to the rules whatever it costs him. Otway's Monimia in *The Orphan*, Southerne's Isabella in *The Fatal Marriage* may innocently be led to disaster, but there is no philosophical implication in these plays, no hint that the sad story presented is evidence of something wrong in the universal frame of things. There may be occasional moments of dubiety, as in Aurengzebe's lines beginning "When I consider life, 'tis all a cheat", but these will occur at random and will not be integrated with the rest of the dramatic statement: after all, *Aureng-zebe* ends happily. In Restoration tragedy, in fact, we see more clearly than elsewhere the lowering of the status of poetry that had come about through the influence of Descartes: it was not the poet's function to pry into the nature of things, that was for the purely intellectual faculty of the philosopher; so that the function of serious drama became, at its lowest, the purveying of the luxury of tears and, at its highest, the sedulous illustration of a traditional scheme of things. It is significant that in the heroic drama we have a serious attempt at a modern dramatic equivalent of the ancient epic, deliberately reflecting traditional notions of right and wrong, of the conduct of the universe. With the drama of his own time Rymer might quarrel when it came to the preservation of the dramatic unities, his keen eye might indeed see many an incidental weakness, but he was not philosophically at odds with his contemporaries as he was with the Jacobeans.

Yet Elizabethan plays continued to be acted in the same theatres as *The Conquest of Granada* and *Venice Preserved*. Not Marlowe, however, and rarely Webster or Ford or Chapman or Tourneur: in tragedy, the Elizabethan heritage was almost wholly confined to the plays of Shakespeare and of Beaumont and Fletcher.[1] The choice is significant, for Beaumont and Fletcher among the leading dramatists of the early seventeenth century are least concerned with the frame of things: like Otway and Southerne they are primarily bent on exciting the kind of emotion that depends on the discouragement of thought. *The Maid's Tragedy* and *A King and No King* shocked Rymer through their violence and fundamental absurdity, they did not provoke him to blind rage as *Othello* did. As for Shakespeare, he might be diluted and amended. The long list of Restoration adaptations of Shakespeare's plays is well known—Dryden's *Tempest*, *Troilus and Cressida* and *All for Love*, Tate's *Lear*, Otway's *Caius Marius* are only the most celebrated—but it is important that several of these adaptations held the stage until the nineteenth century, when Shakespeare had become a national institution, a writer whose language was not always easy to understand and who was in any event to be approached in a spirit of reverence rather than of intellectual enquiry. Indeed, only in this century has it become customary to play Shakespeare's full text, together with the tragic plays of his contemporaries.

These Restoration versions do not merely regularise Shakespeare, they make the plays more acceptable to Thomas Rymer's *Weltanschauung* and his view of the function of poetry. Tate's *Lear* gives to the King and Cordelia a happy ending, Cordelia is recompensed for her sufferings by winning the love of Edgar; Dryden's *Troilus and Cressida* has the alternative title *Truth Found Too Late*: it is a drama of misunderstandings in which Cressida is

---

[1] There were a few performances of other Elizabethan tragedies in the first years of the Restoration, but from the beginning the supremacy of Shakespeare and Fletcher was apparent (cf. Allardyce Nicoll, *Restoration Drama*, 1928, pp. 82–3).

guiltless and Troilus dies a hero's death: Shakespeare's sceptical comedy becomes the kind of play that Fletcher managed with more skill of contrivance.

Edmund Waller, Rymer's most admired poet, even adapted *The Maid's Tragedy* for the Restoration stage. His alteration consisted of the writing of an entirely new fifth act, which makes Evadne change her mind about killing the King and contrives a happy ending for Amintor and Aspatia. Whether or not this version ever reached the stage, it was probably written very near the date of *The Tragedies of the Last Age*: it was published posthumously in 1690, but the strong advocacy of rhyme in the epilogue and the emphasis on the loyalty of the King's brother suggest a date near 1680. It may well be, therefore, that Rymer's animadversions on *The Maid's Tragedy* led Waller to attempt its dilution.

The gulf between Restoration comedy and Restoration tragedy was good for neither. Tragedy, as we have seen, offered a mere excitation of emotion or a piece of embroidery on a conventional frame; comedy became freed from a sense of responsibility and was acceptably adult only in Congreve and in Wycherley's *The Country Wife*. If the tragedy and comedy of an age remain akin, tragedy will maintain contact with the earth and give us real men and women instead of Almanzor and Almahide, will make us look at the human situation without editing; comedy will not show a blindness to the stresses of actuality, will aim at a statement concerning human life and not merely at an evening's libertinage, will have the capacity to produce a *Troilus*, a *Tartuffe*, a *Cherry Orchard*. Certainly in the Restoration period there were many tragicomedies, of which Dryden's *Marriage à la Mode* is the best-known example, where serious heroics and broad jesting alternately occupy the stage. But there is no fusion of comedy and tragedy in them, no realisation that man is at once absurd and magnificent, as there is in Chehov and in Shakespeare. Only Wycherley in *The Plain Dealer* came within measurable distance of writing a comedy with tragic affiliations, and the essential weakness of *The Plain Dealer* is that its serious scenes have no sure basis in a contemporary tragedy: because in his time there was no tragic writing with universal implications, the scenes in which Manly rages and Fidelia droops are merely sentimental.

There can, of course, be tragedy which has no interrelations with contemporary comedy, as in the drama of Athens, but only if there is a strong ritual impulse bringing the play and the audience into close communion. Once the drama becomes less of a communal and more of a personal utterance, then tragedy will either approach nearer to comedy or become merely magniloquent. It is noticeable that the only one of the three tragic writers of Athens who approaches the comic is Euripides, the most individualistic among them. In the Elizabethan and Jacobean years there was a sense of community in the playhouse-audience, though the sense of ritual was far less strong than it had been in Athens: comedy and tragedy existed side by side and drew strength from each other. But in the reign of Charles I we find an increasing emptiness in the tragedies of Shirley, an increasing irresponsibility in the comedies of Davenant: then the reopened theatres of 1660 exhibited a complete divorce between comedy and tragedy, and the way was open for the ranting of Almanzor and the fluttering of Sir Fopling. In the last fifty years we have seen in Chehov, in some of the best of Ibsen and Shaw, in the most persuasive of Mr. O'Casey's dramas, an interplay of comic and tragic attitudes which has given power to the contemporary theatre. In Ireland perhaps we can still find a traditional sentiment so strong that, as in Athens, pure tragedy can hold sway alone: Synge's *Deirdre of the Sorrows* could have no validity apart from a community that had the legend of Deirdre in its blood. The same thing may be true of peasant nations in Europe, but in the urban cultures of England and France and Italy it is difficult to experience the tragic mood without some awareness of its absurdity.

Thus Rymer's objection to the witty exchanges between Iago and Desdemona in II. i of *Othello* points to a weakness in the drama of his age, as does his horror at the tragic *Weltanschauung*.

In this account of Rymer's view of *Othello* we have been led far away from our critic and far away from the play he judged. But perhaps our excursions into a wider field have done something to explain his point of view and its philosophic implications, as well as to underline the basic principles on which Jacobean tragedy resided.

PART II

Chapter 6

"TIMON" AND AFTER

IN this chapter I wish to consider *Timon of Athens* as the starting-point of Shakespeare's last period of dramatic activity, seeing it as containing the germ of the romances, seeing them as in some respects continuing a tendency that *Timon* initiated and in other respects reacting against the cosmic view that *Timon* presented.

In all such matters we find ourselves up against two problems, the problem of chronology and the problem of authenticity. A. C. Bradley [1] and Professor Dover Wilson [2] are united in assigning a date to *Timon* close to that of *Lear*: Timon in his cave, Lear on the heath both rail against humanity, both would level the distinctions that society has laboriously built up, both find treason where they placed trust, both find it difficult to credit that loyalty, in Cordelia and Flavius respectively, may persist. Sir Edmund Chambers, on the other hand, dates *Timon* 1607–8 and sees it as immediately preceding the romances: he speculates 'that during the attempt at *Timon of Athens* a wave (of mental disturbance) broke, that an illness followed, and that when it passed, the break between the tragic and the romantic period was complete'.[3] The exact sequence of Shakespeare's plays must always be a matter of conjecture, but we may remind ourselves that it is not of primary importance: the progression of a man's thoughts is not constant, he may return more than once on his tracks, he may momentarily anticipate a develop-

[1] *Shakespearean Tragedy*, p. 246.
[2] *The Essential Shakespeare*, 1935, p. 131.
[3] *William Shakespeare. A Study of Facts and Problems*, 1930, i. 274.

ment that only much later shows itself fully: *Timon* may precede *Antony* and *Coriolanus* in the actual date of its composition: it does, I think, certainly represent a stage in Shakespeare's development that is logically if not chronologically subsequent to theirs. For the purpose of this chapter, then, I shall treat *Timon* as the point of division between the tragedies and the romances, while being prepared to admit the theoretical possibility that, for example, *Coriolanus* was written later.

In the matter of authenticity, no one is likely to deny the presence of Shakespeare's hand in *Timon* and no one who has read the text can fail to recognise strange inequalities in the level of writing. It may be that Shakespeare was using another man's draft as the groundwork of his play, as he certainly was to do in *Pericles*; it may be that another man intruded his hand into Shakespeare's unfinished manuscript; it may be that we have in *Timon* one of those plays where it is possible to discern the presence of more than one draft of Shakespeare's own composition. Nevertheless, because Shakespeare's hand is indubitably evident at every important moment of the play, I do not think it much matters what theory of *Timon*'s composition we hold to: we can be sure, from what is certainly Shakespeare's, of the general current of his ideas in the treatment of this theme.

The links between *Timon* and some of Shakespeare's other plays of the first decade of the seventeenth century are immediately obvious: between the characters of Lear and Timon we have already seen the link; it is joined to *Coriolanus* and *Antony and Cleopatra* in its use of Plutarch; its Apemantus is cousin-german to Thersites; and Alcibiades' march against Athens inevitably brings to our memory Coriolanus' march against Rome. But in this last particular there is an important difference. Coriolanus marches away, having listened to the pleadings of his

mother: Rome is spared.the brutalities of war at the
expense of its bravest life. Alcibiades meets no Volumnia,
is not even asked to depart by the Senators, but is bidden
only to show mercy and magnanimity in his triumph: this
he willingly consents to, and takes possession of the city.
The Senators' words to him have indeed a high good sense
that gives them validity in other places and times:

> All have not offended;
> For those that were, it is not square to take
> On those that are, revenges: crimes, like lands,
> Are not inherited. Then, dear countryman,
> Bring in thy ranks, but leave without thy rage:
> Spare thy Athenian cradle, and those kin
> Which in the bluster of thy wrath must fall
> With those that have offended: like a shepherd,
> Approach the fold and cull th' infected forth,
> But kill not all together. (V. iv.)

This triumph of Alcibiades at the end of th., play is in
many ways strange. He is a rebel, unjustly exiled it is true,
but ready at once to take up arms against the established
government, asserting his will against the order of the
state, ready in fact to

> Divert and crack, rend and deracinate
> The unity and married calm of states
> Quite from their fixure.

as Ulysses puts it in his 'degree' speech in *Troilus* (I. iii).
No rebuke is ever administered to him for this offence
against 'degree'; Timon will include him in a general
denunciation of humanity but has no special blame for the
friend he has no further use for; Alcibiades enters Athens
as one successful in revolt, in whose hands the reins of
government may lie easily and securely. We are evidently
a long way from the ideas of the history plays, when
usurpation was a dreadful thing, even if the monarch was

scarcely fit to rule, a long way from *Julius Caesar* and even from *Coriolanus*, for there, too, those who would violently transfer authority are seen as necessarily bringing ill to themselves and to the general condition. It is as if Shakespeare is now prepared to see goodness in the domination of a strong man who will exercise his power with benevolence. He is, indeed, distantly approaching the character of Prospero.

But of course the key-position in this play is that of Timon himself, and here we see a marked difference from Shakespeare's previous methods of character-presentation. In his tragedies the central figure is invariably led towards action and disaster by the promptings of other personages in the drama: ¡Othello would not have suspected Desdemona without the agency of Iago; Macbeth would have proceeded no further in the murder of Duncan if his Lady had not steeled him for the task; Lear is precipitated into action through the ready cunning of Goneril and the obduracy of Cordelia; Antony is sinuously entwined by Old Nile herself. In sharp contrast to this, it has been frequently pointed out that Leontes in *The Winter's Tale* feels his jealous agony assisted by no Iago: the passion rises spontaneously within the man, is part of his nature and ready to sprout in due time. It has not, I think, been hitherto noted that Timon resembles Leontes in this: his fatal weakness is the desire for munificent splendour, to which he is incited by no compulsive figure in the play. It would have been easy for Shakespeare to suggest that Alcibiades, knowingly or unknowingly, was the provocation, that to win his regard Timon was straining his purse to pour out the golden rain. But this is nowhere suggested in the play, where Timon indeed stands out against the attempts of Flavius and Apemantus to bring him to his senses, as later he resists the recall to Athens which both Flavius and Alcibiades offer him. This resemblance be-

tween Leontes and Timon points, I think, to a difference
in the conception of character that shows itself generally
in the romances. Earlier Shakespeare had sought always
to give an environmental justification to weakness or vice:
Hamlet's inertia derives partly at least from his reaction
to his mother's re-marriage; Goneril's malignity is to
some extent explicable in view of the behaviour of Lear
in his day of power; Iago had cause enough for envy,
though his morbid condition exacerbated his sense of
grudge. But in the romances characters are good or bad
simply because they are constituted that way. Cloten and
the Queen in *Cymbeline*, Antiochus and his daughter and
Cleon's wife in *Pericles*, Antonio and Sebastian in *The
Tempest*—these are figures as irredeemably given over to
wrong-doing as Imogen and Marina and Miranda are
given up to virtue. In these plays characters may do wrong
and then repent, like Leontes and Posthumus and Alonso,
but—with the minor exception of Posthumus, whose distrust is easily aroused by Iachimo—their wrong-doing is
like a temporary visitation of evil on the soul, not a result
in any degree of environmental pressure. The characters
in *Timon* and the romances lack complexity because of
this: they proceed in a direction that is determined almost exclusively by their own natures. Shakespeare's
latest vision of the world might indeed be described as
peopled by saints and sinners, veering between the poles
of salvation and damnation: no longer is it a world of
interactions, where one man can save or betray another.
Cordelia could bring Lear back to sanity, but Flavius was
sent away from Timon's cave; Iago could twist Othello's
mind towards murder, but the iniquity strong in his
father's court could not lay a finger on the Prince of
Naples.

But of course the general temper of *Timon of Athens* is
far removed from that of the romances: it presents a

quasi-tragic picture of a man's destruction, from which we cannot derive the complete tragic experience because there is not here, as there is in the preceding tragedies, a sense that despite weakness and crime, despite defeat and annihilation, something admirable in mankind is possible. In the murderer Macbeth, in the crazed Lear, even in the woman-ridden Antony, there is a quality of vision, a capacity for stiff-necked endurance, that we juxtapose with the terror that their situation provokes in us. We have seen that tragedy balances terror, the impulse to hide ourselves in the earth and to withdraw from the spectacle, with pride, a feeling of comfort that we share in the humanity of the tragic figure. But we cannot be proud to be of Timon's kin: he is in many ways an imposing figure, with whom we can sympathise, but Shakespeare takes from him any claim to dignity in the later part of the play. Earlier he is foolish as well as liberal, blind to the nature of the situation; later he is reduced to railing, to calling down plagues on his enemies and the world at large. His railing, too, has more of volume than of good sense. He ought to be able to recognise the warm-heartedness of Flavius and the other servants, to see it for his support when at last he realises that Flavius is honest; he should know that Alcibiades was no party to his wrongs; and, moreover, he knew nothing worse than poverty. His humiliation and his misplaced trust were as nothing in comparison with Lear's, yet his curses are as loud. Shakespeare seems to take from Timon the last rag of his self-esteem when he is visited by Apemantus in IV. iii: the cynic who has spent the early scenes of the play in railing against the stupidity of Timon and the rapacity of his followers now comes to see how Timon has reacted to friendlessness; Apemantus offers him no comfort, sees no merit in railing which arises merely from ill fortune, and Timon's reply is to claim a prerogative in his curses be-

cause no other man has known a change of state comparable with his; so they rail on one another, and Timon is
reduced even to stoning his visitor. On the stage this scene
has the temper of savage comedy, for the complete
entanglement of Timon in his circumstances, his inability
to show a mind sharper in vision than Apemantus', makes
us see him as indeed one of the stars' tennis-balls, without
the fortitude that makes even Othello end in dignity. All
he can do is rail, and Apemantus is an older pupil in that
school.

The railing in this play is curiously blunted. Lear in his
madness sees the sufferings of poor naked wretches, unfed
and unhoused in the storm, and he recognises the power
of gold and high place to secure immunity from the
punishment that should by right fall equally on privileged
and unprivileged: Lear in fact sees a rottenness in the
social order, finds nothing sacred in the statutes of
'degree', but his curses are never merely the unpacking
of his heart with words, they represent rather the poisonous but natural fruit of harsh experience. Timon, when he
appears outside the city for the first time in IV. i, asks that
the social order may be overset, not because it incorporates
injustice but because he would wreak his revenge on it,
and then he calls down plagues and fever, sciatica and
leprosy on the city he has spurned: finally he begs the
gods that his hate may grow with the passing of time.
One is reminded of Posthumus' soliloquy in *Cymbeline*,
when he has had the false news of Imogen's adultery: at
the beginning of that speech Posthumus expresses in
forceful, biting words the sense of outrage that he is experiencing: he, like Troilus on an earlier occasion, general-
ises from one woman's infidelity to the corruption of the
whole sex:

> Is there no way for men to be, but women
> Must be half-workers? We are all bastards; all,

And that most venerable man which I
Did call my father was I know not where
When I was stamp'd; some coiner with his tools
Made me a counterfeit; yet my mother seem'd
The Dian of that time; so doth my wife
The nonpareil of this. (II. v.)

His mind is forced to linger on the imagined details of
Iachimo's triumph, and then in a strange anti-climax he
asserts his intention thus:

I'll write against them,
Detest them, curse them. Yet 'tis greater skill
In a true hate to pray they have their will:
The very devils cannot plague them better.

He will in fact turn satirist and find refuge from his pain
in the systematic proclamation of women's evil, just as
Timon will nourish himself on his hatred. There is something adolescent in Posthumus' remedy, as there is something merely currish in Timon's.

On one theme, however, Timon's railing sharpens to
a point. Gold is the source of his overthrow, it is gold that
he discovers in the earth when he is digging for roots, and
the report that once more gold is his brings all his old
followers back in quest of him. He sees it as providing the
over-ruling human motive, the sure lance to break every
law. Looking on the gold he has discovered, he says:

O thou sweet king-killer, and dear divorce
'Twixt natural son and sire! thou bright defiler
Of Hymen's purest bed! thou valiant Mars!
Thou ever young, fresh, lov'd, and delicate wooer,
Whose blush doth thaw the consecrated snow
That lies on Dian's lap! thou visible god,
That solder'st close impossibilities,
And mak'st them kiss! that speak'st with every tongue,
To every purpose! O thou touch of hearts!
Think, thy slave man rebels, and by thy virtue

> Set them into confounding odds, that beasts
> May have the world in empire.   (IV. iii.)

He now recognises it as the one source of his former splendour, and now he welcomes its operations in that its destructive power will surely bring about his revenge on man. There is indeed nothing novel in a Shakespearian tragic figure coming in his grief to a realisation of the evil attributable to gold. Romeo, having heard the false news of Juliet's death and calling on the apothecary to break the law and sell him poison, turns from his own grief for a moment to comment on the deadliness of the metal of traffic:

> There is thy gold, worse poison to men's souls,
> Doing more murders in this loathsome world
> Than these poor compounds that thou mayst not sell:
> I sell thee poison, thou hast sold me none.   (V. i.)

And we saw in Chapter 2 that later the theme was to press more hardly, as in the seventeenth century men became more conscious of the nature of the new society that was coming into being. Lear's thoughts of the poor we have already noted, and he is explicit on the privileges of gold:

> Plate sin with gold,
> And the strong lance of justice hurtless breaks;
> Arm it in rags, a pigmy's straw doth pierce it.   (IV. vi.)

In 1606 Jonson had written *Volpone* and had shown how for money the generality of men will lie and bribe and disinherit a son or traffice in a wife. A few years later he was to take up the same theme in *The Alchemist* and show how the dream of gold would cozen knight and puritan, tradesman and clerk. Later still he was to write a neo-morality called *The Staple of News*, in which the much-wooed heroine is eloquently named Pecunia. And here is Shakespeare writing a play in which gold and its operations provide the motive-force. His central figure is no prince or even a man powerful in the government of the city: it is his wealth and his generosity with it that bring him compliment and treachery. The formal invitation to Timon at the end of the play that he should leave his cave and take up the reins of government seems indeed out of key in a play which is fundamentally based on the experiences of a private man. The story of Alcibiades' successful revolt does not make the play reflect more than incidentally on affairs of state. The minds of serious dramatists at this time were in general turning away from the political to the domestic sphere. I am not thinking only of Heywood's experiments in domestic tragedy but of the more intimate and personal atmosphere that we find in Webster and Tourneur, and later in Ford: these writers make their characters members of princely houses still, but that is partly perhaps due to long-established custom, partly because great place still exercised a compelling fascination: the Duchess of Malfi is primarily a woman, not the ruler of a state; Vindice's 'nest of dukes' that he exterminates are ducal only in their trappings. These writers, it is true, turn their attention to the pathology of sex rather than to the operations of gold, but their neglect of the political theme—the theme par excellence of Marlowe, Chapman and the Shakespeare of the earliest years of the seventeenth century—is still significant. With the increasingly mercantile character of society, it was no longer principality that held the most glorious prize or the sharpest problem: it was man's waywardness in love and his venality. The political struggles of the time are only incidentally reflected by the drama after the first decade of the century, for the men of the theatre were through long habit out of sympathy with the puritanic commons and partially blind to their rising strength.

In Shakespeare's romances there are still kings and

dukes, but the basic situations in the plays are domestic. Cymbeline and Leontes are kings, and they behave at times with the licence which is kingship's prerogative, but their relations with their wives and daughters constitute the main action, despite the Roman war in *Cymbeline* and the courtly settings used in both plays. Prospero is concerned with the business of ruling, but we see him in action with a minimum of subjects: moreover, it is a personal and not a public weal that is, I think, dominantly the concern of *The Tempest*. In turning from the theme of government to the theme of gold in *Timon*, Shakespeare is beginning to explore a path that both he and his contemporaries were to make their own.

On the other hand, *Timon* is in one respect altogether exceptional among early seventeenth-century plays: that is, in its minimal use of women characters. Phrynia and Timandra, the camp-followers of Alcibiades, are the only named women in the play, though a troupe of women masquers appears at Timon's banquet in I. ii. Such women as there are here are treated with scant courtesy, and thus the play stands in marked contrast to those that followed, which in Imogen and Perdita and Miranda have provided many an occasion for rhapsody. At this time most dramatists were giving increasing importance to their women's parts, as for example Webster and Fletcher did; Shakespeare had not long before created Cressida, Lady Macbeth, Desdemona, the three daughters of King Lear, and Cleopatra. Perhaps it was the drawing of Cleopatra with such close analysis of her character that produced a reaction and helped to lead Shakespeare to the choice of a theme where women would for once be unnecessary. Cleopatra, alluring despite her wrinkled brow, capable of grave comfort and genuine grief yet ready to palter with the messenger of Octavius, with immortal longings in her yet pursuing 'conclusions infinite of easy ways to die'(V. ii), had doubtless demanded an exhausting effort of the dramatist's imagination: after her no full-scale portrait of a woman could come from the same pen that would not be an obvious anti-climax. So in *Timon*, the play of railing, women are railed at too—as they were with more appositeness in *Lear*—but they are not with any care depicted. When Shakespeare came to draw women again, it was with the employment of a different method: henceforward it would be the fancy and not the imagination that would be at work. Meanwhile, in the transition play between the tragedies and the romances, there was no need to bother.

It is customary to see *Timon* as the work of a tired man, a man sick in his mind and not yet reconciled with the world. What I have just written may seem to support that view, but the truth about *Timon* is I think more complex. Partly it is a tragedy manqué, failing of its effect because it was no longer possible for the dramatist to feel and to communicate a sense of pride in the central figure he was creating. But partly too it is not the last and least of the tragedies but the doubtful harbinger of the romances, the play which suggests new ideas about the nature of men and how they should be treated, and at the same time points away from the drama of statecraft to the drama of private issues.

When one turns to the romances, one has the sensation of setting a profane foot on sacred territory. Dowden, classifying Shakespeare's dramatic career into four periods, attached the label 'On the heights' to the group of plays consisting of *Pericles*, *Cymbeline*, *The Winter's Tale* and *The Tempest*:[1] though subsequent critics have found his choice of wording sentimental, they have rarely differed much from Dowden in their general appraisal of the last plays. Professor Dover Wilson sees the mature

[1] *Shakspere* (*Literature Primers*), 1931, p. 48.

Shakespeare coming closer to the woods and fields around Stratford, finding in them and in close contacts with his family a kind of Wordsworthian haven.[1] Dr. Tillyard, approaching the matter more soberly, sees in these plays a shifting of stress which is the main source of their difference from the great tragedies.[2] As we saw in Chapter 1, tragedy for him shows the operations of a disruptive force and the final reassertion of normality: thus in the great tragedies the reasonable people—Horatio, Albany, Malcolm, Lodovico—are left in charge of things and the steady current of life is resumed. In the tragedies, this reassertion of normality comes at the very end and is more suggested than expounded; in the romances, it is traced lovingly through its process of development. Thus in *The Winter's Tale* normality appears on the horizon with the beginning of Leontes' remorse in Act III: gradually it rises to the high noon of Hermione's resurrection. We have already considered the view of tragedy implied by this, but the important point in the present context is that it assumes no essential difference between the cosmic view of the tragedies and that of the romances. Moreover, Dr. Tillyard is fundamentally at one with Professor Dover Wilson in seeing Shakespeare concerned in his last group of plays with presenting an optimistic picture of the human situation: troubles come, but they are finally dissipated; at the end humours are reconciled, and there is the peace of resignation and of contentment in the happiness of others. Mr. Wilson Knight puts forward a more startling assessment of the last plays: we are to see them, he says, not 'as pleasant fancies' but rather 'as parables of a profound and glorious truth', finding their place after the problem plays and the tragedies in the same way as the *Paradiso* follows the *Inferno* and the *Purgatorio*, as indeed

[1] *The Essential Shakespeare*, pp. 134–45.
[2] *Shakespeare's Last Plays*, pp. 16–26.

the resurrection of Christ follows his temptation in the desert and his ministry and death.[1] This would appear a strange judgment on the plays that include the brothel-scenes of *Pericles* and the jealous agony of Leontes, the railing of Posthumus and the intrigues of Antonio and Sebastian, the characters of Cloten and Caliban and the acrid fooling of Trinculo. It overlooks, too, the stage-manager's delight in scenic device that shows itself often in these plays, particularly in Paulina's exhibition of the statue and Prospero's revelation of Ferdinand and Miranda at chess. And it disregards the affinity with Fletcher's style in verse and characterisation, particularly the echoes of *The Faithful Shepherdess* that find their way into *The Tempest*.

Not one of these theories seems to be an adequate explanation either of the plays themselves or of their relation with *Timon*. Nor does the impish account of the matter given by Lytton Strachey in his essay on 'Shakespeare's Final Period'. He would have us believe that, by the time of the romances, Shakespeare was 'bored to death', turning out plays to meet the popular demand for wide-canvas tragicomedy, and at times putting superb poetry in them through long-established habit.[2] But the striking things in the romances are not merely splashes of fine verse, like Florizel's apostrophes to Perdita: they include much that is clearly the result of prolonged and profound thought, like the brief disquisition on nature and art that Polixenes gives to Perdita in the sheep-shearing scene of *The Winter's Tale* (IV. iii). And, whatever one's reaction to *The Tempest*, one cannot dismiss it as a play lightly undertaken and casually executed: whatever its significance, it was one that was deeply at home in Shakespeare's mind.

Yet marks of casualness in this last group of plays there

[1] *The Crown of Life*, 1947, pp. 30–1.
[2] *Books and Characters*, 1922, p. 60.

undoubtedly are, and they are most evident in the earliest of the group, *Pericles*. As it stands this is a botched affair, and not even Mr. Wilson Knight can claim to find Shakespeare's hand in the whole of it.[1] The commentators are generally agreed that Shakespeare took over another's work and that his hand becomes clearly discernible from the third act. Moreover, Shakespeare's use or preservation of the Gower chorus passages seems, partly at least, to stem from a disinclination to make the story tell itself, though partly too Shakespeare may have desired the effect of greater distance between spectators and actors that the intervention of a narrator effects. In any event, Thaisa's withdrawal to the temple of Diana seems over-hasty: even in the ill-defined days of the play's action, communication between Tyre and Ephesus cannot have been altogether unknown. Perhaps after *Timon* Shakespeare was undecided how to proceed: in that play he had shown signs of weariness and of a general contempt for the nature of mankind. If he could have been left to himself, a longer interval might have come before he resumed his pen. But he was his company's most successful dramatist, he was a sharer in their gains, and doubtless it was difficult for him to resist the clamour for more theatre-stuff. A dramatic romance, by Wilkins or another, lay at hand, at least partially written but woefully unready for playing. The solution of his and the company's problem could be found in setting to work to manipulate another man's material. Had not Greene long ago accused him of filching? It was a habit that might be conveniently resumed. Nevertheless, his writing in the completed *Pericles* was sufficiently extensive to make the presence of his hand beyond question and to constitute the play a minor landmark in his development. In it we have clear anticipations of what he was to write later and we have too an extension

[1] *The Crown of Life*, p. 32.

of certain characteristics that had first become noticeable in *Timon*.

We get, for example, a black-and-white method of characterisation. On the one side, Pericles, Marina, Thaisa, Cerimon; on the other, Antiochus and his daughter, Dionyza, and the keepers of the brothel in Mitylene. The good are incorruptible, so that Pericles can quickly throw off his love for the daughter of Antiochus as soon as he guesses at her sin, and Marina comes no nearer harm than Milton's Lady in *Comus*. And the characters of the bad are not explored but merely exposed: Boult the pandar is not humanised like his cousin Pompey in *Measure for Measure*, he is simply not of Pericles' kin, the dark strain in the world which sets off the light. It is true that Boult is finally won over to Marina's plan for her livelihood and agrees to spare her from the fellowship of the brothel, but that appears only for the convenience of the plot: after he has dropped his demands on her, his character is dropped by the dramatist: it has served its turn, to be Marina's foil, and Shakespeare has no further use for or interest in it. We may come to understand the nature of the last plays if we direct our attention closely to the treatment in them of those who have sinned: sometimes, like Leontes and the enemies of Prospero, they are forgiven, but first they are most rigorously tormented; more often, they get no forgiveness but a sharp condemnation. The clearest example in *Pericles* is provided by the presentation of Cleon, the governor of Tarsus, whose wife Dionyza plotted the death of Marina through jealousy: Cleon was ignorant of the plot, and is horrified when the news of Marina's murder is given him: his fault is that he does not denounce his wife and acquiesces in the deception of Pericles. This might be thought an almost pardonable fault, but it is worth while our noticing the references to him in the last act of the play: in scene i, line 173, he is 'cruel Cleon', in line 218 'savage Cleon', in line 254 'inhospitable Cleon'; in scene iii Pericles accuses him of seeking to murder Marina, and in Gower's concluding chorus he is 'wicked Cleon' and we are told that the people rose against him and burned "him and his" in his palace. The reader may conjecture that here we have careless workmanship, a forgetfulness on Shakespeare's part of Cleon's comparative guiltlessness. But this is surely improbable, and indeed the variety of the abusive epithets that are attached to Cleon's name in the last act even suggests a special animus against the character. It is because Cleon has condoned his wife's fault, has not applied the salutary discipline of a Prospero, that he comes under rebuke.

Dr. Tillyard has noted that when Marina 'preaches' in the brothel-scenes we 'end by thinking her a prude'.[1] Yet, just as in *Measure for Measure* we are amazed that the half-nun Isabella should turn on Claudio with the suggestion that her mother must have played her father false and with the accusation that his desire to live makes him guilty of a kind of incest (III. i), so here it is startling that Marina uses such imagery as this in her abuse of Boult:

> Thou art the damned door-keeper to every
> Coystril that comes inquiring for his Tib,
> To the choleric fisting of every rogue
> Thy ear is liable, thy food is such
> As hath been belch'd on by infected lungs. (IV. vi.)

But while Isabella's excesses provide a clue to the kind of woman that Shakespeare is presenting in her, Marina's direct our attention, not to her character, but to the state of mind of its creator. This kind of speaking is to be found in Timon's mouth, as he rails indiscriminately against human nature. It is the product of a sharp revulsion from

---

[1] *Shakespeare's Last Plays*, p. 23.

the tolerance of the early plays: Marina becomes Shakespeare's medium for reviling: she lashes the pandar with her words as Paulina does to Leontes and Prospero to all who have offended him. We see the triumph of Alcibiades in a clearer light through this: 'degree' was hardly sacred any more, men and their society should be made to feel the whip.

In matters of detail, *Pericles* anticipates the later romances very noticeably. In II. i, which may well be Shakespeare's, three Fishermen converse on the storm and the wreck they have just seen: the situation and their expression of pity point to Miranda's:

> *Third Fisherman.* Faith, master, I am thinking of the poor men that were cast away before us even now.
> *First Fisherman.* Alas! poor souls; it grieved my heart to hear what pitiful cries they made to us to help them, when, well-a-day, we could scarce help ourselves.

And from the wreck came Prince Pericles, a stranger to the land, who would marry its Princess, as later there came Ferdinand for Miranda. In II. v Simonides abuses Pericles as Prospero abuses Ferdinand, each with the same intent, to ensure the wedding of his daughter; Thaisa, moreover, is as forward in admitting her love as Miranda was to be, and Simonides pretends anger with his daughter as Prospero with his. In III. i Lychorida rebukes Pericles on shipboard with "Patience, good sir; do not assist the storm", sending our minds forward to the Boatswain's "You do assist the storm" in the opening scene of *The Tempest*. The presentation of Cerimon's character in III. ii is a kind of preliminary sketch for Prospero's: both have studied the secrets of nature through their books and learned to do strange things. One might list such resemblances at length, linking the appearance of Diana here with the descent of Jupiter in *Cymbeline*, the frequent references to the passing of time in Gower's speeches with the very appearance of Time as chorus before Act IV of *The Winter's Tale*, the reviving of the apparently drowned Thaisa with the animating of Hermione's statue, the omnipresence of the sea in this play with the island setting of *The Tempest*. What should emerge from such a list is the realisation that Shakespeare, stumbling upon this form of play in the rehandling of another man's work, found it much to his purpose and decided to continue in the same path.

Yet doubtless he would not have continued if *Pericles* had not proved popular. How it pleased its audience we know from a curious mention of it on a curious occasion. In 1613—four or five years after the writing of *Pericles*— certain London apprentices took over the Whitefriars theatre to act Robert Tailor's play *The Hogge hath lost his Pearle*. For some obscure reason—perhaps because the Hog of the play was thought to be a portrait of the then Lord Mayor, Sir John Swinnerton—the sheriff's officers interrupted the performance and carried six or seven of the players to prison.[1] Nevertheless, the play was printed, together with a prologue which indicates the amateur status of the performers and concludes in this way:

> Wee are not halfe so skild as strowling Players,
> Who could not please heere as at Country faiers,
> We may be pelted off for ought we know,
> With apples, eggs, or stones from thence belowe;
> In which weele craue your friendship if we may,
> And you shall haue a daunce worth all the play.
> And if it prove so happy as to please,
> Weele say tis fortunate like *Pericles*.

This is testimony not merely that the fame of *Pericles* had lasted for a few years but that it could be rather

[1] Cf. E. K. Chambers, *The Elizabethan Stage*, 1923, iii. 496.

condescendingly alluded to, as Ben Jonson might refer to *The Spanish Tragedy* or *Titus Andronicus*. That should not surprise us, for by 1613 Beaumont and Fletcher's tragicomedies had established themselves on the stage, and in technical competency *Pericles* would look strange beside them. It is for us important, seeming to advance Shakespeare on the road from *Timon* to *The Tempest*, but for its contemporaries it might be simply one of his less impressive displays, carelessly put together and a little childish in its flights of fancy. Nevertheless, it pleased.[1]

Cymbeline and *The Winter's Tale* demanded more care in the writing, but Shakespeare had found his new métier and consequently the impetus to composition had come back. The stories he uses are echoes of the past: *Cymbeline* is like *Lear* in its ancient British setting and in the estrangement between the King and his virtuous daughter; in the gulling of Posthumus by Iachimo it has an obvious relation to *Othello*; *The Winter's Tale*, apart from its general resemblance to *Pericles*, also echoes *Othello* in Leontes' jealousy and attempted murder of his Queen. But if Shakespeare is prepared to re-work old situations, it is in their development of his new way of writing that these plays are important. Again we have portraits of vice and virtue clearly distinguished: the virtuous, like Posthumus, may err, but they will be made to suffer sharply before they are allowed forgiveness and safe harbour. The vicious, like Cloten and the Queen, are exterminated without a pang as they are drawn without a humanising trait. Iachimo is certainly pardoned in the end, when we might have expected a severer fate for him; but it was convenient for him to repent and to provide the puzzled British court with an explanation of the strange conduct

---

[1] For the view taken of *Pericles* by Caroline audiences, see the quotation given below, p. 172, from Tatham's commendatory verses to Brome's *A Joviall Crew*.

of events: when Posthumus gives him his quittance, it is
casually and condescendingly done:

> Kneel not to me:
> The power that I have on you is to spare you;
> The malice towards you to forgive you. Live,
> And deal with others better.   (V. v.)

There is perhaps an unconscious irony in Cymbeline's
comment on this:

> Nobly doom'd:
> We'll learn our freeness of a son-in-law;
> Pardon's the word to all,

for pardon is not for the dead Queen and Cloten: there
are limits in this play to the orbit of forgiveness. In *The
Tempest* Prospero was to go further, but the play of *Cymbeline* has not been so thoroughly thought out. The business of the Roman wars is a complication hardly justified,
and Cymbeline's reception of the news of his wife's death
is presented as if Shakespeare did not care to hide his
indifference to this part of his subject: the King's first
comment is that it ill befits a doctor to bring news of
death, but then he reminds himself that we all are mortal;
when the doctor tells him the dying Queen in her final
delirium proclaimed that she had never loved her husband and tha she had poisoned Imogen, Cymbeline's
simple comment is:

> O most delicate fiend!
> Who is't can read a woman? Is there more?   (V. v.)

Indeed, while we need not accept Lytton Strachey's view
that in the romances Shakespeare was almost continuously
indifferent to the plays he was writing, we can admit that
in certain places he relaxed visibly at his task.

Not, however, with the character of Imogen. There we

can recognise a strenuous care to win the audience's sympathy and to express an ideal. In the former aim he has been clearly successful, in the latter frequently misunderstood. Imogen is no Rosalind, despite her male attire: she is akin rather to the significantly named Castabella of Tourneur's *The Atheist's Tragedy*, which was written about this time. Like Fletcher, but with a deeper because more morbid passion, Tourneur idealises chastity here, while at the same time eagerly imagining its defilement. We are again indebted to Dr. Tillyard for drawing attention to the strange comment of Posthumus on his wife, in the passage already quoted from, where he rails upon her supposed defection: [1]

> O! vengeance, vengeance;
> Me of my lawful pleasure she restrain'd
> And pray'd me oft forbearance; did it with
> A pudency so rosy the sweet view on't
> Might well have warm'd old Saturn; that I thought her
> As chaste as unsunn'd snow.   (II. v.)

This would be altogether puzzling if we did not relate it to the violent revulsion from the body that had appeared already in *Timon* and *Pericles* and was to show itself most clearly of all in *The Tempest*. In a different way the puritanic tinge of Shakespeare's latest phase appears also in *The Winter's Tale*. There, as we have seen, Polixenes argues with Perdita on the subject of art and nature, urging her not to scorn the 'streak'd gillyvors', for grafting and other artificial processes, coming from man and his knowledge of nature, come ultimately from nature herself. Perdita's reply is to persist in the cult of simplicity:

> I'll not put
> The dibble in earth to set one slip of them;

---

[1] *Shakespeare's Last Plays*, p. 31.

No more than, were I painted, I would wish
This youth should say, 'twere well, and only therefore
Desire to breed by me.   (IV. iii.)

The victory in argument belongs to Polixenes, but the
dramatist's sympathy seems to lie with the unpainted girl,
the untouched and uncontrived bloom. It is not sentimental, because it appears to go deep into the writer's
inclinations: it is a further exalting of the good, and a
warning of taboo.

In *The Winter's Tale* there is more vitality, more joy,
than in either *Cymbeline* or *The Tempest*. Autolycus is the
last of Shakespeare's comic figures to win our sympathy—
for I doubt very much whether Trinculo and Stephano
contrive that—and the whole of the sheep-shearing scene
is in its lyrical kind unmatched. The puritanic strain is all
the sharper for the appreciation of the delights of life, as it
is also for the understanding of Leontes' jealous agony.
We are made to feel that Leontes is punished, not so much
for driving Hermione towards death, as for letting his
mind dwell so persistently on sexual possession and loss.
Only in that way can we come near understanding
Paulina's continual stirring of his memory: as it is, an
audience is likely to turn against the monitress and to view
with something like alarm her marriage with Camillo at
the end of the play. That Shakespeare should not have
anticipated such an audience-reaction goes to suggest that
his attitude towards guilt at this time—and particularly
guilt bound up with sensuality—was not the common
attitude. Because Paulina's utterance was his own, he was
unaware of its harsh monotony.

These plays, then, are of haphazard structure, exempli-
fied notoriously in the convenient devouring of Antigonus,
with the craftsmanship of individual scenes varying from
the highest to almost the lowest, with lyrics and lyrical
blank verse finer than ever before, with repulsive scenes

and characters juxtaposed with Whitsun pastorals and elaborate theophanies, with a sharp delight in nature and human beauty mingling with an urge to the discipline of man's unruly flesh. The diverse elements remain unco-ordinated as yet. *The Tempest* was to brew them in a single cauldron, with a magician's craft.

Chapter 7

"THE TEMPEST"

THE puritanic strain which I have spoken of as discernible in the later plays of Shakespeare is not without parallel among the playwrights who were his contemporaries. Notably Marston and Tourneur rail against the weaknesses of the flesh with a comparable ferocity, and with them as with Shakespeare we feel that there is strong tension between the impulse to indulgence and the impulse to restraint. I have already instanced Tourneur's *The Atheist's Tragedy*, with its heroine Castabella as at once an image of purity and an incitement to lust: Marston's *The Dutch Courtezan* shows the conflict of impulses differently, displaying the courtezan Franceschina in her remarkable attractiveness and in her tempting of Malheureux to murder his friend. In both these plays there is some direct presentation of puritanism: *The Atheist's Tragedy* has a comic puritan, Languebeau Snuffe, as the central figure in its sub-plot, and Malheureux before his captivation by the Dutch courtezan is puritanically inclined. Both Tourneur and Marston dislike the puritan bias even when most evidently under its sway. One of the reasons, in fact, for the mental disorder which characterises so much of Jacobean drama is that the writers were searching for principles of morality while at the same time resenting the strongest moralisers of their day. The contrast with the contemporary drama in Spain is most evident: there, though there could be touches of rebellion on a dramatist's part, as when Tirso de Molina can hardly resist admiring his damned Don Juan, yet the fabric of religion was established and acceptable. The Jacobeans, on the other hand, had no rock for their feet and, when the virtuous fit was on them, could only swim desperately between the deep waters of a pagan stoicism and the quicksands of a prurient negation. Hence their most puritanically inclined plays would contain a burlesque portrait of a puritan or would show the writers fascinated by the lechery they proscribed. Hence Marina's presence in a brothel, which gives a piquancy to the character's effect while at the same time displaying her virtue. Hence, too, the problem of Caliban in *The Tempest*.

Shakespeare's early references to puritanism are by no means flattering. All the world knows Sir Andrew Aguecheek's reaction when Maria reports that Malvolio is said to be a puritan (II. iii), and Sir Toby's indignant rejection of household discipline:

> Dost thou think, because thou art virtuous, there shall be no more cakes and ale? (II. iii.)

The dialogue between Angelo and Escalus in *Measure for Measure* does, moreover, put a plea for toleration: Angelo defends the condemnation of Claudio for his irregular liaison with Juliet; Escalus petitions the Lord Deputy to be merciful and urges that the possibility of fault is within every man. This passage is eminently quotable because directly and dispassionately it contrasts the attitude of the man who thinks himself one of the elect, proof against assault, and that of the man who sees humanity as one kin, each man subject to the effects of circumstance:

> *Angelo.* We must not make a scarecrow of the law,
> Setting it up to fear the birds of prey,
> And let it keep one shape, till custom make it
> Their perch and not their terror.
> *Escalus.* Ay, but yet
> Let us be keen and rather cut a little,
> Than fall, and bruise to death. Alas! this gentleman,

Whom I would save, had a most noble father.
Let but your honour know,
Whom I believe to be most strait in virtue,
That, in the working of your own affections,
Had time coher'd with place or place with wishing,
Or that the resolute acting of your blood
Could have attain'd the effect of your own purpose,
Whether you had not, some time in your life,
Err'd in this point which now you censure him,
And pull'd the law upon you.
    Angelo. 'Tis one thing to be tempted, Escalus,
Another thing to fall. (II. i.)

Immediately afterwards the two men sit in judgment on Pompey the bawd: since Elbow the constable is his accuser and Pompey himself is not the easiest of witnesses to handle, the proceedings become amusingly fantastic: Angelo loses patience and leaves Escalus alone in charge: he, with firmness and good humour, manages the affair as one who knows human nature and is not shocked by it. Here, as later in the play with Angelo's overthrow, Shakespeare appears to reject the puritan's attitude towards human nature, and to suggest that a tolerant handling of evil-doers is not only wiser but more in accord with the conditions of human existence. So long as a man feels kinship with the vicious and the weak, he is likely to counsel mercy; when he strives, perhaps with incomplete success, to think of some men as among the elect and others as outside the fold, he will demand sharp penance even from the elect and, for the others, often the utmost rigour of the law.

It was almost inevitable that the puritanic strain should manifest itself in Shakespeare as soon as he found it difficult to maintain the tragic attitude. So long as the world could be seen as dragging a tragic figure to destruction, leading him to error and crime through the effect of its impact on him, yet incapable of destroying his sense of his own being—"I am Antony yet," cries Antony in his disgrace—so long was it possible for Shakespeare to retain faith in human nature as having the stuff of goodness in it. When the world appeared no more evil than man himself, then Shakespeare like Tourneur turned his curses on men. Even in *Measure for Measure* the final punishment of Lucio, ridiculous as it is, has something of spite in it, and the spite is not wholly the Duke's. In *King Lear* we find Edgar's comment to his dying brother Edmund: he sees the misery of their father as springing from the dissolute begetting of Edmund, and pronounces that

> The gods are just, and of our pleasant vices
> Make instruments to plague us:
> The dark and vicious place where thee he got
> Cost him his eyes.   (V. iii.)

The terrible justice of the gods will seize, it appears, upon a small fault and exact a dreadful retribution. It is hardly in tune with a humane view of things that the eyes of the libertine should be plucked out. This extreme of remorselessness attributed to the gods is a hint of the spirit underlying the romances. It is not surprising that Shakespeare's puritanic recoil should be violent, for he has left us plenty of evidence of a strong sensuality in his earlier writings. James Joyce put a convincing case in *Ulysses* that *Venus and Adonis* was no mere exercise in a fashionable mode,[1] and Shakespeare could not have drawn the lovers in *Romeo and Juliet* or in his comedies if his sympathy with them had not been warm. Moreover, it can hardly be coincidental that the theme of infidelity is ever-recurrent in his plays, as it is indeed the impelling force in many of his sonnets. It may be lightly enough treated in *The Two Gentlemen of Verona*, but in *Much Ado*, in *Hamlet* and in *Troilus* there is a growing intensity in its handling. In

[1] *Ulysses*, 1947, p. 179.

these plays, as in *Othello* and *Lear*, the almost-physical agony of loss is given to us to share. Sometimes we are dealing with actual infidelity, as in Gertrude's to her dead husband and her living son, Cressida's to Troilus, Goneril's to Lear, sometimes with the mere supposition, as with Claudio in *Much Ado*, Othello, and Lear in his mistrust of Cordelia. But in all alike we have a passion for possession, and a corresponding ache when their arms are empty. It is the more passionate nature that seeks in time for the curb upon itself, as Miss Helen Darbishire suggests was Wordsworth's case.[1] So that Shakespeare's puritanism when it came had the strength of his earlier passions, and Prospero is drawn with the same bold outlines as Falstaff.

I have no wish to use other evidence than the plays in order to trace the currents in Shakespeare's mind, but the biographically curious may think it worth noting that in 1614 a visiting preacher to the town of Stratford was entertained at New Place: Sir Sidney Lee thought the man was probably a puritan, and connected his visit to Shakespeare's house with the known puritan sympathies of John Hall, Shakespeare's son-in-law.[2] We may observe too that, if there is anything in the statement of Richard Davies, a Gloucestershire parson of the late seventeenth century, that Shakespeare 'dyed a papist',[3] there is no need to find this contradictory to speculations about his puritanism. No one would attempt to suggest that Shakespeare identified himself in his last plays with the doctrines of any particular sect: his puritanism was of the sort that any man rebellious against his own flesh may come to, and it is by no means incompatible with the possibility

---

[1] *Wordsworth. Poems in Two Volumes. 1807*, edited by Helen Darbishire, 1914, p. xxvi.

[2] *A Life of William Shakespeare*, 1915, p. 466.

[3] E. K. Chambers, *William Shakespeare*, 1930, ii. 257.

that before death he returned to the form of religion which he had known in his earliest childhood: Dr. J. H. de Groot has put it beyond doubt that Shakespeare's father kept to the older religious practices.[1] The plays, of course, show no precise doctrine, though their anti-humanism has a Calvinist tinge.

One approaches *The Tempest* with some diffidence because of the aura of sanctity with which so much allegedly critical writing has invested it. All the romances seem generally to inhibit thought in their readers, but, while one may safely find inequalities in the other three, to lay a finger on *The Tempest* is, even to-day, almost to declare oneself worthy of the heretic's fire. Nevertheless, a casual scrutiny should assure us that here is a play with strange features. It is about a man who neglects his dukedom—in that way deserving stern rebuke from the Elizabethans, who had stringent demands to make on a ruler, who saw the defection of Gorboduc and Richard II and Lear as blameworthy and the source of inevitable woe. Yet nowhere is Prospero blamed for this, and he is allowed to win a greater power in place of his dukedom and, more blessed than other deposed princes, to wreak sharp vengeance on all who were associated with his deposition. Perhaps the Duke in *Measure for Measure* resembles him a little, for he too could desert his post at a critical moment and could resume power most magisterially at the end of the play. Indeed there are anticipations of the later plays here and there in *Measure for Measure*, for already Shakespeare was turning from a firm belief in 'degree' and an interest in the social order to an almost exclusive concern with private issues. In *The Tempest* Prospero's duty as Duke of Milan is altogether secondary: what matters here is his command over those of his immediate circle on the enchanted island, and they are not so much citizens of a

[1] *The Shakespeares and 'The Old Faith'*, 1946.

commonwealth as men subject to another's, and a higher, will. Indeed, the remoteness of the play's atmosphere from the common air of earthly principalities is evident from a few words in Prospero's farewell to his magic: outlining the achievements that his art has known, he includes the statement that

> graves at my command
> Have wak'd their sleepers, op'd, and let them forth
> By my so potent art. (V. i.)

As we know that no one has been raised from the dead on the enchanted island, Professor Schücking claims this as an example of 'episodic intensification', the device which he suggests Shakespeare employs to heighten the effect of a particular scene or passage even at the expense of con-tradiction with other sections of the play.[1] Mr. Kenneth Muir and Mr. Sean O'Loughlin have pointed out that the whole passage from which these lines are taken is closely modelled on some dozen lines from Golding's translation of Ovid,[2] and the implication would appear to be that Shakespeare took over the idea from his model (where it appears simply as "I call vp dead men from their graues") without thought or care for the fact that we know of no resurrection achieved by Prospero. Yet in this play we can hardly imagine that Shakespeare was so carefree. *The Tempest* is nothing if not planned. Even the unusual pre-servation of the unities of time and place is symptomatic of Shakespeare's self-discipline here. The catalogue of Prospero's magical achievements goes beyond the letter of fact because in this play symbolism everywhere dis-places verisimilitude. We are not dealing here with a duke who has failed in his task of ruling, but with a man who has laboriously won the power to discipline others, who has become as a god, a god who scourges.

---

[1] *Character Problems of Shakespeare's Plays*, p. 115. Cf. above, p. 97.
[2] *The Voyage to Illyria*, 1937, p. 40.

In his earlier years Shakespeare wrote a play of magic in *A Midsummer Night's Dream,* and there are superficial resemblances to that play here. There a king of the fairies who can set mortals a-wandering; here a magician who can dazzle or lead astray or terrify his visitors. There a mischievous sprite in Puck, obedient to Oberon; here Ariel, bound to his master's will. There a group of common men providing earthy comedy in the enchanted setting; here Trinculo and Stephano giving their cue for laughter. But the wood has Athens near, while the island is remotely at sea. In *A Midsummer Night's Dream* we know the dawn will come and the lovers will be home again; in *The Tempest* we cannot imagine Miranda as Queen of Naples or Prospero again a common duke. If the early play finds its key-utterance in Puck's "What fools these mortals be!" (III. ii), *The Tempest* is supremely articulate in Prospero's comment: "Some of you there present Are worse than devils" (III. iii).

Certainly Prospero is no easy task-master. Ariel, begging for freedom, enrages him: the docile spirit is called 'malignant thing' and is made to call to memory all the torments it endured through the witchery of Sycorax. And such torments, it is threatened, may be renewed:

> If thou more murmur'st, I will rend an oak
> And peg thee in his knotty entrails, till
> Thou hast howl'd away twelve winters.   (I. ii.)

All his old enemies Prospero delights to terrify, and in the exercise of his power he does not spare his old friend and helper in need, Gonzalo, until even the non-human Ariel is impelled to intercede for them:

> The king
> His brother, and yours, abide all three distracted,
> And the remainder mourning over them,

Brimful of sorrow and dismay; but chiefly
Him, that you term'd, sir, 'The good old lord Gonzalo':
His tears run down his beard, like winter's drops
From eaves of reeds; your charm so strongly works them,
That if you now beheld them, your affections
Would become tender.   (V. i.)

Ferdinand he abuses and humiliates, because indeed he
must learn to prize the Miranda who has been magically
thrust upon him. Nowhere can we find a parallel to the
love-scenes between Ferdinand and Miranda, so carefully
contrived by the master of them both, so exultantly eavesdropped. When the girl is dazzled at the appearance of
the young prince, Prospero delights in the working of his
schemes: "It goes on, I see, As my soul prompts it," he
says (I. ii). And when Ferdinand, addressing Miranda,
refers to 'the Duke of Milan and his brave son' as among
those lost in the shipwreck, Prospero's aside is:

The Duke of Milan
And his more braver daughter could control thee,
If now 'twere fit to do't.   (I. ii.)

Then again, when he sees affection springing, his comment is:

They are both in either's powers: but this swift business
I must uneasy make, lest too light winning
Make the prize light.   (I. ii.)

In his view there must always be discipline and the hours
of toil, with Miranda as the half-holiday at the end of the
week. When Miranda enters to find Ferdinand bearing
his logs, Prospero is present with them, secure in his
invisibility. Of his daughter he comments:

Poor worm! thou art infected:
This visitation shows it.   (III. i.)

And at the end of the scene his admission "So glad of this

as they, I cannot be, Who are surpris'd withal" underlines the lovers' lack of free choice. In the sultry atmosphere of the enchanted island even young love is engineered.

Prospero treats the 'poor worm' his daughter in most schoolmasterly fashion in I. ii, punctuating his story of his loss of Milan with frequent questions to test the intelligence of his pupil and with continual injunctions that she should pay attention. Throughout the play, indeed, he is a kind of celestial schoolmaster who teaches obedience to his will and considers that his pupils have profited, if only in that. He will deceive them without remorse, making Ferdinand believe his father dead, and Alonso the same of his son. Even at the end of the play, when he has decided that "The rarer action is in virtue than in vengeance", he delights to keep Alonso in ignorance of Ferdinand's preservation and in riddling speech mocks his grief by pretending that his own daughter is likewise dead:

> *Alonso.*　　If thou beest Prospero,
> Give us particulars of thy preservation;
> How thou hast met us here, who three hours since
> Were wrack'd upon this shore; where I have lost,—
> How sharp the point of this remembrance is!—
> My dear son Ferdinand.
> 　　*Prospero.*　I am woe for't, sir.
> 　　*Alonso.*　　Irreparable is the loss, and patience
> Says it is past her cure.
> 　　*Prospero.*　I rather think
> You have not sought her help; of whose soft grace,
> For the like loss I have her sovereign aid,
> And rest myself content.
> 　　*Alonso.*　　You the like loss!
> 　　*Prospero.*　As great to me, as late; and, supportable
> To make the dear loss, have I means much weaker
> Than you may call to comfort you, for I
> Have lost my daughter.

Alonso.   A daughter?
O heavens! that they were living both in Naples,
The king and queen there! that they were, I wish
Myself were mudded in that oozy bed
Where my son lies. When did you lose your daughter?
    Prospero. In this last tempest.   (V. i.)

Then he appears to dismiss the subject, like a conjurer misdirecting his audience's attention, so that it comes as a greater surprise a few lines later when he draws the curtain and shows Ferdinand and Miranda at chess. It is the celestial stage-manager at work once more, as it was when Paulina exhibited the statue at the end of *The Winter's Tale*. The prize is awarded after the period of discipline, but the almighty contriver must be allowed his thrill in building up his effect.

But of course it is in his treatment of Caliban that Prospero's lack of human sympathy is most clearly shown. After he has told Miranda his story and given Ariel his instructions and his morning lesson in obedience, he awakens Miranda from the sleep that he has cast on her and oddly suggests: "We'll visit Caliban my slave, who never Yields us kind answer." Miranda is reluctant to join in this kind of sport, but she is easily overridden. When Caliban comes obedient to the summons, Prospero makes free use of the word 'slave' and is liberal with his threats. Thus:

> For this, be sure, to-night thou shalt have cramps,
> Side-stitches that shall pen thy breath up; urchins
> Shall forth at vast of night, that they may work
> All exercise on thee: thou shalt be pinch'd
> As thick as honeycomb, each pinch more stinging
> Than bees that made them.   (I. ii.)

And in valediction this:

> If thou neglect'st, or dost unwillingly
> What I command, I'll rack thee with old cramps,

Fill all thy bones with aches; make thee roar,
That beasts shall tremble at thy din.   (I. ii.)

Later Caliban tells us more of the ingenious devices of his
master:

His spirits hear me,
And yet I needs must curse. But they'll nor pinch,
Fright me with urchin-shows, pitch me i' the mire,
Nor lead me, like a firebrand, in the dark
Out of my way, unless he bid 'em; but
For every trifle are they set upon me:
Sometime like apes, that mow and chatter at me
And after bite me; then like hedge-hogs, which
Lie tumbling in my bare-foot way and mount
Their pricks at my foot-fall; sometime am I
All wound with adders, who with cloven tongues
Do hiss me into madness.   (II. ii.)

When, ultimately, Prospero turns his canine spirits on
Caliban and his companions, he bids Ariel see that the
tormenting is done soundly:

Go, charge my goblins that they grind their joints
With dry convulsions; shorten up their sinews
With aged cramps, and more pinch-spotted make them
Than pard, or cat o' mountain.   (IV. i.)

Mr. George Garrett in his lively essay 'That Four-flusher
Prospero' has commented on the apt names, 'Fury' and
'Tyrant', of two of Prospero's dogs.[1] At the end of the
play Caliban is presented by his master to Alonso, and his
words are strangely significant: "this thing of darkness I
Acknowledge mine" (V. i). The acknowledgement gives
us indeed the clue to Prospero's extravagant rancour towards his slave. Caliban, in Prospero's eyes, is humanity
in all its vileness: he represents the untamed beast, un-

[1] William Empson and George Garrett, *Shakespeare Survey*, n.d.,
p. 62.

amenable even to the sharpest discipline. When Prospero first came to the island, he was prepared to use its single inhabitant with kindness, but the dark strain in Sycorax' whelp choked benevolence. During the time of the play's action, we find Prospero unpacking his heart with words of hate and striving to sate an unappeasable hunger for revenge. But why revenge? Many readers of the play have been puzzled by the extent of Prospero's disturbance in IV. i: he interrupts the masque with which the lovers' betrothal is being celebrated, and both Ferdinand and Miranda comment on his appearance of distress:

> *Ferdinand.* This is strange: your father's in some passion
> That works him strongly.
> *Miranda.*   Never till this day
> Saw I him touch'd with anger so distemper'd.

Then follows the famous speech on the mutability of all things—which indeed is entirely a-christian in its equation of life with a dream and death with sleep—and then Prospero comes back to the moment with a kind of apology for his disturbed condition:

> Sir, I am vex'd:
> Bear with my weakness; my old brain is troubled.
> Be not disturb'd with my infirmity.
> If you be pleas'd, retire into my cell
> And there repose: a turn or two I'll walk,
> To still my beating mind.

Yet it was an easy task for the magician to put down the petty revolt of Caliban and the fine specimens of manhood with whom he was now associated. At every point in the development of their plot, Ariel is present and ready to do Prospero's will: in the result a few gaudy rags are instruments enough for their overthrow. We can explain Prospero's initial change in his treatment of Caliban only by turning back to I. ii, where we are told what action of

Caliban led to his exile from the fellowship of Prospero and Miranda. There, when Caliban claims that the island has been stolen from him, Prospero's reply is:

> Thou most lying slave,
> Whom stripes may move, not kindness! I have us'd thee,
> Filth as thou art, with human care; and lodg'd thee
> In mine own cell, till thou didst seek to violate
> The honour of my child.

This assault on Miranda is indeed a recurrent theme in the play: Caliban rejoices in the memory of it, and the possession of Miranda is the climax of the inducements that he offers to Stephano in persuading him to kill Prospero (III. ii). Caliban speaks throughout the play in blank verse: he is aware of beauty, whether in Miranda or in the fair features of the island or in music or his dreams, but there is no moral good in him: he learns nothing through Prospero's discipline and is finally led to repent his rebelliousness only because Prospero looks so fine in his ducal robes and because Stephano's drunken incompetence is at length too manifest to escape even Caliban's attention. The character is presented with a kind of reluctant pity, as if despite his later self Shakespeare cannot fully overcome his sympathy with the common strain in man. Even in *Pericles* the pandar Boult shows an occasional touch of this, but Caliban is a full-length portrait which Shakespeare strives to detest while at the same time suggesting a nostalgia for his latitudinarian days. When Shakespeare was presenting Falstaff in the Second Part of *Henry IV*—a more deeply considered play than Part I— he could be aware of the ills of the flesh while being free with his sympathy in the depicting of a gross epicurism. Falstaff spoke in the prose of common life, and Shakespeare presented him as a good boon-companion, to be joyfully wondered at so long as affairs of state were not too pressing. But Caliban speaks in verse, because now the depicting of sensual man is a reminiscence as well as a theme for castigation. *The Tempest*, carefully planned as it is, is written not from one point of view but from two: it is at once a sermon on discipline and a half-appalled, half-fascinated recalling of the past. Caliban in his assault on Miranda is not wholly outside Shakespeare's orbit of sympathy, just as Tourneur's D'Amville in *The Atheist's Tragedy* partially reflects the dramatist's impatience with what Castabella symbolises. And for that very reason Caliban must be tormented and D'Amville must die.

The point is made clearer by the behaviour of Prospero at the betrothal of his daughter. He accompanies his consent to the wedding with a solemn charge that Ferdinand shall not anticipate the nuptial ceremony:

> Then, as my gift and thine own acquisition
> Worthily purchas'd, take my daughter: but
> If thou dost break her virgin knot before
> All sanctimonious ceremonies may
> With full and holy rite be minister'd,
> No sweet aspersion shall the heavens let fall
> To make this contract grow; but barren hate,
> Sour-ey'd disdain and discord shall bestrew
> The union of your bed with weeds so loathly
> That you shall hate it both: therefore take heed,
> As Hymen's lamps shall light you.   (IV. i.)

No young man could behave with more sedateness and decorum than Ferdinand does, and his reply is an emphatic acceptance of the terms. But twenty lines later, after Prospero has sent Ariel to prepare the masque, he returns to the subject in his preceptor's fashion:

> Look, thou be true; do not give dalliance
> Too much the rein: the strongest oaths are straw
> To the fire i' the blood: be more abstemious,
> Or else good night your vow!

This time Ferdinand's reply seems embarrassed, and is without doubt embarrassing to any actor who must repeat his words:

> I warrant you, sir;
> The white-cold virgin snow upon my heart
> Abates the ardour of my liver.

As if that was not enough, the charge is implicitly conveyed a third time in the masque itself, when Iris assures Ceres that Venus and her son will not be present at these rites, although they at first planned to do mischief with 'some wanton charm'. No behaviour could be more impertinent, in the full sense of the term, than Prospero's here, and it cannot be understood other than pathologically. As it happens, we can make an illuminating comparison between Prospero's behaviour and that of Friar Lawrence in a not dissimilar situation. In *Romeo and Juliet* the lovers have met at the Friar's cell and freely express the tumult of their passion. Friar Lawrence's brief comment on this concludes the scene:

> Come, come with me, and we will make short work;
> For, by your leaves, you shall not stay alone
> Till holy church incorporate two in one.   (II. vi.)

He is a prudent man, who will see to it that the forms of Holy Church are decently observed, but he does not seize on the opportunity for a sermon, as we may remember that Parson Adams did when Joseph Andrews grew impatient to wed his Fanny:[1] the Friar here knows his human nature and is prepared to mingle prudence with a reasonable indulgence. The forms are necessary, but he will 'make short work' of them. There could be no clearer illustration of the difference in temper that the passing of fifteen years had wrought in Shakespeare.

[1] *Joseph Andrews*, Book IV, chap. VIII.

Shakespeare's preoccupation with the theme of infidelity shows itself curiously at one moment in this play. It is in V. i when Prospero has drawn the curtain and discovered the lovers at chess. If it were possible to imagine Shakespeare as facetious here, one might be amused at the prudence of their occupation, with the chess-board between them, but that is by the way. What is strange, and I think significant, is their brief snatch of dialogue before they realise the presence of others:

> *Miranda.*   Sweet lord, you play me false.
> *Ferdinand.*   No, my dearest love,
> I would not for the world.
> *Miranda.*   Yes, for a score of kingdoms you should
>   wrangle,
> And I would call it fair play.

It would have been so easy for Shakespeare to have invented a fragment of conversation more appropriate to the chess-table than an accusation of cheating. The charge of falseness is intrusive here, and seems to force its way into the play because somehow or other it must flow from Shakespeare's pen. It may be a legacy from the sonnet-period, but, if so, it was one that long endured and is particularly noticeable when it is irrelevant to the dramatic action. It is worthy of observation here because Shakespeare's puritanic inclinations in his latest plays seem partly to derive from his obsession with the infidelity theme.

But if Prospero must rage against Caliban as the spirit of the earth, he will threaten with bonds too the unbridled fancy, the personification of free-ranging poetic thought. Ariel must be correspondent to command and do his spiriting gently: there is always the possibility of his rebellion, of the poetic faculty taking the law into its own hands. The puritan poet must always distrust the vagrancy of his own blood. So we can explain the unmeasured wrath of Prospero when Ariel begs for early release. There will be liberation, or abandonment, before long, but until then all must be in the master's control. Yet Shakespeare could no more forget the songs of an earlier time than he could entirely put from him the inclusive charity and good-fellowship that had helped him to imagine Falstaff and Lucio and Othello. So Ariel in this play is a resilient sprite, avid for fun and mischief when Prospero's frown is not on him. And in the end it is Ariel who urges Prospero to have mercy on his enemies, it is the poetic fancy that finds a link with humanity before the stern judgment has relaxed. We might almost be driven to interpret *The Tempest* as a mere allegory of the wronged man's need to acquire the faculty of forgiveness, were it not that the concluding scenes of the play repel us with their recurrent harshness of tone and their burden of moral exhaustion.

At the end indeed, as at the end of *Cymbeline* and *The Winter's Tale*, there is a general pardon. The treachery of Antonio and Sebastian is not revealed to Alonso, and Caliban, Trinculo and Stephano are contemptuously despatched to Prospero's cell, with the recommendation that Caliban should 'trim it handsomely' if he wishes to escape further punishment. There is a perplexing casualness about it all. Prospero addresses the company with "Welcome! my friends all", and then adds aside to Sebastian and Antonio:

> But you, my brace of lords, were I so minded,
> I here could pluck his highness' frown upon you,
> And justify you traitors: at this time
> I will tell no tales. (V. i.)

One would have thought that a brother prince should warn Alonso of the danger that he has been in from these men and that he may well be in again, but Prospero is content to 'tell no tales'. There is no reconciliation here, or repentance. Antonio is still 'most wicked sir', and he does not speak in this scene except to add a single line to the baiting of Caliban. And the poor monster is still 'this thing of darkness', to be given no good words and to be shown as repenting nothing more than his imprudence. The conclusion, in fact, gives one the impression that the task of disciplining human nature had grown wearisome to contemplate, had been recognised as impossible to execute. Prospero's tired and sententious epilogue, in which he asks for prayer, suggests that his abandonment of the schoolmaster-magician's robe is significant of Shakespeare's own sense of the futility of castigation. His victims were, after all, projections of himself, and at length the flagellant drops his scourge and tries to pray. The exercise has been unprofitable, for the flesh and its vices are as strong as ever. Because *The Tempest* gave the fullest and most ordered expression of the puritan impulse in Shakespeare, and because when it was done the world seemed as it was before, it seems likely that the traditional view is correct that Shakespeare wrote no later complete play. *The Tempest* was no testament, it was a sign not of peace but of continuing war and a great weariness that, after the maximum effort, things must be as they had been. Prospero will go back to Milan, will think of death, and meanwhile will see the old world around him—with Antonio and Sebastian ready to resume their plots if a favourable opportunity arises, as it will for them or others like them, and with Caliban the living symbol of man's lust and defiance of the law.

That this play has largely inhibited critical thought in its readers and spectators seems evident from the fact that most people are ready to laugh at the Trinculo and Stephano scenes. Certainly *The Tempest* is a painful work to analyse, and hence the effort to believe that it is much as Shakespeare's earlier comedies with a dash of mysticism thrown in. Yet one must stand amazed at the customary reception in the theatre of the so-called 'comic' scenes. Of course, Shakespeare was still the dramatic practitioner, and he meant these scenes to give variety and a cue for laughter. Moreover, there are moments when the dialogue of Trinculo and Stephano is as good as is customary in a music-hall of the second class. Yet here surely we find the weariness of temper that appears also in the play's conclusion and epilogue. The playwright cannot summon up sufficient interest in his butler and jester: they have none of the touches of humanity that animate so many of Shakespeare's clowns from the Launce of *The Two Gentlemen of Verona* to the Autolycus of *The Winter's Tale*. Moreover, the contrast between their cluttered prose and Caliban's ever fanciful blank verse inevitably makes our attention leave them. Then, too, Shakespeare by chance or with extraordinary perspicacity has made their relations with Caliban so apt a comment on the relations of colonisers with natives. Wretched as they are, they can dazzle him, can give him strong drink and the illusion that they will free him from an old servitude. His gods totter as the world widens for him, and he exults in a new liberty, until he discovers the folly of worshipping them and their inability to better his condition. Meanwhile he is humiliated in being so easily deceived and in paying homage to the riff-raff of the civilised world. Swift's diatribe on colonial policy at the end of Book IV of *Gulliver's Travels* is no sharper in its satire than these scenes become when Caliban is led by the nose. We feel something more painful than embarrassment when, at the end of II. ii, he sings drunkenly and cries out: "Freedom, high-day! high-day, freedom! freedom! high-day, freedom!" After all, Trinculo and Stephano are the emissaries of our world. And if it is argued that Shakespeare would not have been sensitive to such things, that for him it would be as amusing to make a native drunk as to make a Jew turn Christian, we may remind ourselves that his sympathy was widespreading: did not Isabella remind Claudio that

> the poor beetle, that we tread upon,
> In corporal sufferance finds a pang as great
> As when a giant dies? (III. i.)

Many readers thus have come to regard the fates of Shylock and Caliban with grave discomfort. And the comic scenes of *The Tempest*, intended to lower the status of Caliban still further, to make him an object of mockery as well as detestation, have served with some of us to sharpen our sense of him as the one character in the play whose kin are to be found in the plays of the middle period. And this could hardly have happened unless, with one part of his mind, Shakespeare had seen him as we do.

But if the comic prose of *The Tempest* is defective, the verse is not. Solemn and musical at once, moving with grace from the lyrical to the contemplative, from narration to invocation, it gives at the same time an impression of having been wrought with much labour. This, we have seen, is no play dashed off, as *Pericles* may well have been, as in comparison even *Cymbeline* and *The Winter's Tale* doubtless were. The play was to give concrete and final expression to the condition of stress which the dramatist knew in his mind: its structure shows careful forethought, as does indeed the fabrication of its story and the juxtaposition of its characters. So too the verse shows grace without ease, hard-won artifice with no warbling of native wood-notes. We may note the deliberateness of such lines as:

> Where should this music be? i' th' air, or th' earth?
> It sounds no more;—and sure, it waits upon
> Some god o' th' island. Sitting on a bank,

Weeping again the king my father's wrack,
This music crept by me upon the waters,
Allaying both their fury and my passion,
With its sweet air: thence I have follow'd it,
Or it hath drawn me rather,—but 'tis gone.
No, it begins again.   (I. ii.)

No marvel that Mr. Eliot has held these lines so retentively and has woven them into place in the verse of *The Waste Land*. There is gravity here, with as it were a yearning for the delights of ear and eye, like that which Mr. Eliot writes of in the third section of *Ash Wednesday*, a poem on penance like *The Tempest*. The songs and the references to music and the tempered sweetness of much of the verse show a glimpse of the purified world which Shakespeare the puritan might reach out to in his dreams. But the play as a whole shows also how the world looked to him awake. Like *Timon of Athens*, *The Tempest* is a play about a man who abandons power and the practice of chastisement, and in neither case does the abdication bring content. "Sun, hide thy beams! Timon hath done his reign" are the last words spoken by the Athenian; the returning Duke of Milan tells us in his epilogue that, unless the help of prayer is given to him, his 'ending is despair'. The progress from the one play to the other may be a slow groping after religious consolation, though Prospero's equation of sleep and death suggests that the groping is not over. Assuredly, too, the plays of the last period trace the development of a new ethical attitude. But the end is not peace, neither with nature nor with men.

Chapter 8

THE CAROLINE AUDIENCE

DR. I. A. RICHARDS, examining the nature of 'meaning', has drawn attention to the importance of 'tone', i.e. the relationship between writer and reader which is suggested through the writer's manner of utterance.[1] Certainly one of the most difficult barriers to negotiate is that set up by a wrong tone in something we hear or read. When the writer has us in view as among his potential audience, he is to be blamed for the erection of the barrier: he should find a way of reaching us if he knows he has something to tell us. But a writer of the past or of another nation than our own is not usually addressing us: his public is very different in its attitudes, conventions, acceptances, and it is to them that his tone must primarily be adapted. Consequently, in our judgment of past literature, we have always to consider the public addressed: we may then see why the tone of a literary work is not the one we most delight in, and may be prepared to recognise that this tone was apt in its context. We may still reject the work for another reason, but at least we shall be saved from condemning an eavesdropped conversation because its language is not our own.

This matter of tone becomes particularly important in dramatic studies. We cannot enter a theatre without to some extent partaking of a group-consciousness, which will make our demands on, and expectations from, the dramatist more rigid than are our isolated demands and expectations in private reading. But theatrical expectations vary greatly from one age to another, from one kind

[1] *Practical Criticism*, 1930, pp. 182, 206-9.

of theatre to another. Athens in the age of Pericles and London in the reign of Charles II produced theatres which were about as far apart as theatres can be, and the expectations of the two audiences consequently differed. A dramatist cannot work without some consideration, even if scornful, of his audience, and his 'tone' will arise from his attitude to their expectations. In trying to reach a correct understanding, therefore, of the drama of any period, we must try first to appreciate the character of its audience: only by knowing that so well that we can discount it shall we be able to follow the playwright's meaning unchecked by oddity of tone.

In using 'tone' in this way, we must think not of mere turns of phrase in a dramatist's speech, but of the whole design, temper, embellishments of his work. These, quite as much as the individual words and sentences, are affected by the relations of writer and audience. The chorus, the static quality, the reticence of Greek drama constitute part of its 'tone', just as that of Restoration comedy is indicated by its use of songs, its artificial balancing of characters, as well as by its tricks of speech. Everything that is part of the medium of communication will be inevitably affected by the writer's attitude to his public, will contribute to the 'tone' of the whole work.

The drama of Charles I's reign has especially suffered through insufficient attention to its audience. The change from the democratic, widely gathered audience of Shakespeare's time to the aristocratic audience of the Restoration is well known, and it is of course recognised in books on the subject that this change was a gradual one, that Caroline audiences were often courtly,[1] but it should be far more generally recognised that many Caroline plays were written for an entirely different public from the

[1] Cf. Allardyce Nicoll, *The English Theatre*, 1936, pp. 74–5; Alfred Harbage, *Cavalier Drama*, 1936, pp. 19, 149.

popular Elizabethan one. The emotional refinement of Ford and Shirley, the compromises of Davenant, the sense of unease in Massinger, the constant impatience of Brome —are all to be traced to the context in which their plays grew. The audience had not the post-War and post-Interregnum characteristics of the Restoration theatre-public: it was a society that delighted in a new-won gentility, that played a little clumsily with its new toys. Masques and plays were for these people a way of escape from the unpleasantness of political circumstance and a means of cultivating the graces. The popular theatre which they patronised was not, of course, capable of the splendours of Whitehall, but still it could spin a charming story to its two-hours' length. Some of the dramatists, like Shirley, might move towards the attitude of calm appraisal that marks the Restoration, and some, like Massinger, might feel more kinship with a robuster, earlier age, but the keynote of the years was inattentiveness. The spectators could thrill to a new horror or to a love endangered, but their minds strayed from an idea. Ford is a master-poet in spite of his time, though his lesser qualities are Caroline through and through: the playwright closest to the age is Davenant, who could offer noisy rant, competent satire, or dilute pathos, and never be wholly serious about it.

It is difficult not to take an *ex post facto* view, but the Caroline audience seems like a community of people waiting for its own dissolution, sipping its hemlock daintily.

Of course, not all theatrical entertainment in Charles's time was politely patronised. The Red Bull and the Fortune continued to provide rougher fare for city stomachs, but the Blackfriars, Salisbury Court and the Phoenix were all 'private'—i.e. enclosed—theatres with a genteel character.[1] It is for these fashionable playhouses that nearly all

[1] Alfred Harbage, *Cavalier Drama*, p. 149.

the famous plays of the time were written,[1] and we are therefore justified in regarding this audience as the typical Caroline one. In ruder amphitheatres something more strictly Elizabethan survived, but this is almost as uncharacteristic of the age's theatre as the survival of mystery plays till the end of the sixteenth century is un-Elizabethan.

It may be questioned whether the reign of Charles I can rightly be called a 'period', and indeed one must readily admit that all the characteristics of the drama and its audience that we find in the years 1625–42 are anticipated earlier in the century. There is no major revolution in 1625, but in the years that follow it is evident that slow changes have transformed the Elizabethan theatre. Spectacle, romantic tragicomedy, hesitant gentility of speech and action, make their appearance in Jacobean plays, as do the characteristics of the audience that brought these things into demand, but Charles I's reign can claim

---

[1] Shirley's *The Doubtful Heir* (1640) was intended for the Blackfriars but actually played at the Globe, and it is interesting to find the dramatist doubting its suitability for the vast open theatre: it has

> No shews, no dance, and, what you most delight in,
> Grave understanders, here's no target-fighting
> Upon the stage, all work for cutlers barr'd;
> No bawdry, nor no ballads; this goes hard;
> But language clean; and, what affects you not,
> Without impossibilities the plot:
> No clown, no squibs, no devil in't. . . .
> But you that can contract yourselves, and sit
> As you were now in the Black-friars pit,
> And will not deaf us with lewd noise and tongues,
> Because we have no heart to break our lungs,
> Will pardon our vast stage, and not disgrace
> This play, meant for your persons, not the place.
>
> (Prologue.)

Here Shirley is being over-complimentary to the Blackfriars public, who liked spectacle in their own refined way, but the reference to the more intimate style of Blackfriars acting is significant.

rank as a dramatic 'period' because of two things: the new refinement of the court materially affected the drama of the playhouses; and a new school of writers, who came directly under this influence, took on the task of playwriting from their elders. The Queen had a passion for masques and plays, for seeing, 'producing' and acting in them, and her taste was imposed at court. Courtly amateur writers invaded the playhouses, and carried there the Queen's jurisdiction. The professional writers developed their craft in a new atmosphere, which prescribed gentility. Fletcher died in 1625: he was the Jacobean writer most akin in his temper to the Caroline playwrights, and, though his work seemed old-fashioned to them, they followed his methods and wrote prologues for revivals of his plays. Others of the elder dramatists survived into Charles's reign, but only Jonson stood out against the new temper, and his contempt for the age he had lived into was answered with rebuke. Heywood went on writing with his genius for acclimatisation, working the Caroline vein as he had worked earlier ones. Chapman had nothing to give the newer drama. In the place of these men, there arose a group of five outstanding playwrights in the middle twenties of the century, who were to write the best plays of Charles's time. Massinger was working from the beginning of the decade; Shirley, Davenant, Ford and Brome began their careers almost simultaneously with the new reign. It is significant that Massinger was the earliest of them, for he has the strongest links with the Elizabethans. But together they represent a new 'school', which had taken over the task of directing English drama, and their style and temper are sufficiently removed from those of earlier years to warrant our inspecting Charles's reign as a separate dramatic 'period'.

In searching the play-books of the time for indications of the audience's character, we shall find most of our evidence in the prologues and epilogues. These direct addresses necessarily take their tone from the spectators even more obviously than the plays themselves: they are intimate where the earlier prologues and epilogues were impersonal and aloof, and time and again they offer us detailed descriptions of, and comments on, the persons addressed.[1] The epilogue to Fletcher's *Wit at Several Weapons* (1609), spoken 'at the reviving of this Play' after Fletcher's death, glances at the fine-clothed gentlemen and the befanned ladies who are now gathered to see it:

> We'll not appeal unto those Gentlemen
> Judge by their Cloaths, if they sit right, nor when
> The Ladies smile, and with their Fanns delight
> To whisk a clinch aside, then all goes right.

Brome's *The Court Beggar* (1632) has a long prose epilogue in which the ladies, the courtiers and the citizens are addressed in turn by different speakers. Shirley makes his prologue-speaker to *The Coronation* (1635) address the ladies as the reigning goddesses of the playhouse, whose nod gives victory:

> But what have I omitted? Is there not
> A blush upon my cheeks, that I forgot
> The ladies? and a female Prologue too!
> Your pardon, noble gentlewomen, you
> Were first within my thoughts; I know you sit,
> As free, and high commissioners of wit,
> Have clear, and active souls, nay, though the men
> Were lost, in your eyes, they'll be found again;
> You are the bright intelligences move,
> And make a harmony in this sphere of love.

---

[1] There are signs that the custom of prologues and epilogues fell into comparative disuse in the earliest years of the century: cf. above p. 50. The resurrection of the prologue, with the change in its character, is itself an indication of the change in audience.

And this polite romance has an epilogue in which Shirley repeats his appeal:

> If smiles appear within each lady's eye,
> Which are the leading stars in this fair sky,
> Our solemn day sets glorious; for then
> We hope, by their soft influence, the men
> Will grace what they first shined on.

Davenant's *News from Plymouth* (1635) was acted at the Globe during a vacation, and the prologue rejoices that fine clothes and polite judgments are there to greet the King's Men in their less exclusive summer-resort:

> A noble company! for we can spy,
> Beside rich gaudy sirs, some that rely
> More on their judgements than their clothes, and may,
> With wit as well as pride, rescue our play:
> And 'tis but just, though each spectator knows
> This house, and season, does more promise shows,
> Dancing, and buckler fights, than art or wit.

But not every vacation-prologue is so confident. Glapthorne's *Poems* of 1639 contains a prologue "To a reviv'd Vacation play" which addresses itself to the citizens who have been left to fill the theatre in summer: the poet is anxious to believe that these spectators can appreciate dramatic wit and tries to cajole them into living up to his good opinion:

> You are our daily and most constant Guests,
> Whom neither Countrey bus'nesse nor the Gests
> Can ravish from the Citie; tis your care
> To keep your Shops, 'lesse when to take the Ayr
> You walke abroad, as you have done to day,
> To bring your Wives and Daughters to a Play.
> How fond are those men then that think it fit
> T' arraigne the Citie of defect of Wit?

When we do know, you love both wit and sport,
Especially when you've vacation for't.
And now we hope you've leisure in the Citie
To give the World cause to suspect you witty.

The picture of the audience in the prologue to Sir Aston
Cokain's *The Obstinate Lady* (1639) is thoroughly Restoration in tone: gentlemen, he says, come to find wenches or
to sleep after food and drink, wantons to look for clients,
ladies to meet their cavaliers. He takes up a rather for-
bidding attitude towards such debasements of the theatre
—though his own plays are hardly attractive enough to
warrant more serious patronage—but his main interest
for us is his recording of them. But indeed we have other
evidence of polite bad manners in the playhouse. As early
as 1606 Beaumont's *The Woman-Hater* has a picture of
the fine gentleman who enjoys the murmuring of "What
Nobleman is that?" as he enters, while all the gallants on
the stage rise to offer him their seats (I. iii).[1] Later a
gallant could enjoy female admiration too: Cowley's *Loves
Riddle* (1633) has this comment on fine clothes:

doe you thinke your glorious sute can fright me?
'Twould doe you much more credit at the Theater,
To rise betwixt the Acts, and looke about
The boxes, and then cry, God save you Madame.   (III. i.)

This graceful gesticulating to the boxes had its humbler
parallel: Glapthorne in *Wit in a Constable* (1639) speaks of

city foremen
That never dare be ventrous on a beauty,
Unlesse when wenches take them up at playes
To intice them at the next licentious Taverne
To spend a supper on them.   (II. i.)

But there is no doubt from which quarter the tone was set:

---

[1] Quoted by Allardyce Nicoll, *The English Theatre*, p. 74.

the boxes were addressed most intimately by prologue-speakers, the common folk superciliously.

These gentry of the boxes were not content to exhibit themselves: they stooped to the art of criticism, and the playwright, wincing under the lash, often rebuked them for their arrogance in his prologue and epilogue. The author's retort to criticism appears, of course, earlier in the century, but now it becomes more frequent and directed more against the two-sexed fop [1] than against the malicious censurer. Marston, who has much to say of critics, speaks as to stray antagonists: in the induction to *What You Will* (1601) he gives us a long discussion of the spectators' expressions of disapproval, and of authors' contempt for them; in the prologue to *The Dutch Courtezan* (1603) he recognises the presence of enemies:

> As for some few, we know of purpose here
> To taxe, and scout.

So, too, in his prologue to *Parasitaster, or The Fawne* (1605):

> Let those once know that here with malice lurke,
> Tis base to be too wise, in others worke.

And in the epilogue he reasserts his scorn for

> Malitious censures of some envious few,
> Who thinke they loose if others have their due.

But the earlier audience had robust common sense as well as occasional malice, as Fletcher readily acknowledges in *The Captain* (1610):

> If a marriage should be thus stubber'd up in a play, e're almost
> Any body had taken notice you were in love, the Spectators
> Would take it to be but ridiculous. (V. v.)

---

[1] Even the foppish critic, however, was not new: Jonson had attacked the species in the induction to *Cynthia's Revels* (1600).

Certainly it is a convenient device to persuade an audience to accept an odd turn of plot by reminding them of its very improbability, but the testimony to their quick-wittedness, however disingenuous, was wrung from Fletcher by their actual keenness of response. When we turn from these retorts to consider the situation of the Caroline playwrights, we find a mixture of real contempt with flattery. The dramatists knew often enough how shallow were these brocaded judgments, yet not all dared to be other than civil. Jonson, of course, cared little about courtship, and his induction to *The Magnetick Lady: or, Humors Reconcil'd* (1632) is blunt:

> *Dam.* But the better, and braver sort of your people! Plush and Velvet-outsides! that stick your house round like so many eminences—
> *Boy.* Of clothes, not understandings? They are at pawne. ... Troth, Gentlemen, I have no wares, which I dare thrust upon the people with praise. But this, such as it is, I will venter with your people, your gay gallant people: so as you, againe, will undertake for them, that they shall know a good *Play* when they heare it; and will have the conscience, and ingenuity beside, to confesse it.

But Ford, in the epilogue to *The Broken Heart* (1629), cunningly differentiates between the shallow commentators and the genuine understanders:

> Where noble judgments and clear eyes are fixed
> To grace endeavour, there sits truth, not mixed
> With ignorance; those censures may command
> Belief which talk not till they understand.
> Let some say, "This was flat"; some, "Here the scene
> Fell from its height"; another, "That the mean
> Was ill observed in such a growing passion
> As it transcended either state or fashion":
> Some few may cry, "'Twas pretty well", or so,
> " But—" and then shrug in silence.

The imagined comments are those of fine folk, as empty
of wit and as full of jargon as the stop-watch and stock-
term criticisms that Sterne found so irking.[1] Davenant,
less bold to burlesque his critics' phrases, could attack
'the over-subtle few' who show 'Some easy wit but much
more cruelty' in the prologue to *Love and Honor* (1634),
could fearfully remind himself that spectators 'are grown
of late, harsh and severe' in the prologue to *The Platonic
Lovers* (1636), could assure the gentlemen, in his epilogue
to *The Unfortunate Lovers* (1638), that they had his consent to 'rail at all' while their 'wives and country friends'
found only 'a fault or two in every act'. But in the prologue
to *The Unfortunate Lovers* he speaks out more plainly,
contrasts the present cavilling spectators with their easily
satisfied predecessors, and gives us a detailed account of
the progress of the theatre from Elizabethan *naïveté* to
Caroline sophistication:

> you are grown excessive proud,
> For ten times more of wit, than was allow'd
> Your silly ancestors in twenty year,
> Y' expect should in two hours be given you here;
> For they, he swears, to th' Theatre would come
> Ere they had din'd to take up the best room;
> There sit on benches, not adorn'd with mats,
> And graciously did vail their high-crowned hats
> To every half dress'd Player, as he still
> Through th' hangings peep'd to see how th' house did fill.
> Good easy judging souls, with what delight
> They would expect a jig, or target fight,
> A furious tale of Troy, which they ne'er thought
> Was weakly written, so 'twere strongly fought;
> Laught at a clinch, the shadow of a jest,
> And cry a passing good one, I protest.
> Such dull and humble-witted people were
> Even your fore-fathers, whom we govern'd here;

---

[1] *Tristram Shandy*, Book III, chap. XII.

And such had you been too he swears, had not
The poets taught you how t' unweave a plot,
And tract the winding scenes, taught you to admit
What was true sense, not what did sound like wit.
Thus they have arm'd you 'gainst themselves to fight,
Made strong and mischievous from what they write.

There is something of Restoration vanity here: already
the writer looks back to a barbaric past, and sees his own
age as one of refinement. The chains of an exacting public
were sometimes galling, but his very abuse has a more
than civil leer. There can be little doubt whence this refinement came: the theatre, as Shirley indicated in the
prologue and epilogue to his *The Coronation*, derived its
doctrine from women's eyes. Davenant himself describes
a critical lady in *The Fair Favourite* (1638) as one to whom
the 'poets bow' because 'she is so critical' (IV. ii). Such
influence operated in a way not unknown in our contemporary London theatre: a new author's name was dis-
trusted, long plays were disliked, some spectators came to
hear rather than see, others to see rather than hear, others
in plenty only to be seen. That indeed is what Glapthorne
tells us in the prologue to *The Ladies Priviledge* (1637),
trembling lest his play too should have the "pitious
Martyrdome" that so many suffered from those lithe-
figured judges. Shirley, ever the courtier, is critical of
critics in his prologue to *The Imposture* (1640), but concludes with an assurance of devotion to the ladies:

To the ladies, one
Address from the author, and the Prologue's done:
In all his poems you have been his care,
Nor shall you need to wrinkle now that fair
Smooth alabaster of your brow; no fright
Shall strike chaste ears, or dye the harmless white
Of any cheek with blushes: by this pen,
No innocence shall bleed in any scene.

If then, your thoughts secur'd, you smile, the wise
Will learn to like by looking on your eyes.

Before this he had condemned the 'poetic schism' that 'A prologue must have more wit than the play', lamented the decaying craft of the playwright, and bid the gentlemen 'choose your way to judge' without understanding 'too little or too much'. All might be corrected and rebuked except brows of alabaster and eyes that sometimes smiled.

To discover what kept those brows smooth and those eyes sympathetic one has only to read the plays of Charles's time, to see the cult of the vicarious thrill in tragedy, the pleasing long-drawn sigh of tragicomedy, the depiction of current absurdity in comedy. But prologue, epilogue and commendatory verses again give us information directly. The playwrights knew what was happening: though their ranks were on occasion swelled by courtier-amateurs, they were for the most part men of the theatre who had grown up under Shakespearian, Jonsonian and Fletcherian influences; they knew their own pedigree, and had sometimes the wit to be proud of it. Thus Thomas Carew, writing commendatory verses for Davenant's *The Just Italian* (1629), laments the bad taste of those who prefer current Red Bull and Cockpit fare to the art of Beaumont or Jonson, and Tatham in verses commending Brome's *The Joviall Crew: Or, The Merry Beggars* (1641) sees Jonson, Beaumont, Fletcher, Shakespeare all brought down in current estimation. Tatham, indeed, warns the spectators against this heresy, just as Dryden was later to remind his readers that an attack on Shakespeare and Jonson was an attack on 'our poetical church and state': [1]

There is a Faction (Friend) in Town, that cries,
Down with the *Dagon-Poet*, *Johnson* dies.

[1] Dedication to *Examen Poeticum* (1693).

171

His Works were too elaborate, not fit
To come within the Verge, or face of *Wit*.
Beaumont and *Fletcher* (they say) perhaps, might
Passe (well) for currant Coin, in a dark night:
But *Shakespeare* the *Plebean* Driller, was
Founder'd in's *Pericles*, and most not pass.[1]
And so, at all men flie, that have but been
Thought worthy of Applause; therefore, their spleen.
Ingrateful *Negro-kinde*, dart you your Rage
Against the Beams that warm'd you, and the Stage!

The muscularity of early dramatic exercise they rejected
for an etiolated gracefulness of word and movement. But
at court this gracefulness was splendidly accoutred, and
they brought to the common playhouse a demand for
spectacle. Inigo Jones was not there to overwhelm the
poet with his rich embroidery, but there were devices to
hold the eye. Not surprisingly, Jonson could protest, as
he makes his prologue-speaker do in *The Staple of News*
(1625): the actors, he says, must provide shows for those
who come to see rather than hear, but the playwright dis-
claims responsibility for such accretions to his work. So,
too, an elder dramatist like Heywood assures his audience
in the prologue to *The English Traveller* (1627) that drums,
trumpets, dumb shows, songs, dances and masques are
here eschewed: there have been so many in that kind that
he wishes on this occasion to try 'if once bare Lines will
bear it'.[2] He speaks less patiently in *Loves Maistresse: Or,
The Queens Masque* (1636), where Apuleius says he will
keep Midas awake by a dance of Vulcan and his Cyclops,
for "The Vulgar are best pleas'd with noyse and showes"
(IV. iii). This gibe is oddly placed in *Loves Maistresse*,
a spectacular fancy in which Heywood ministered nicely
to later taste, but the homespun bareness of this man's wit

---

[1] Cf. above, p. 132.

[2] He had expressed himself rather similarly in the much earlier prologue
to *A Woman Kilde with Kindnes* (1603).

made him at times feel discomfort in the context of his old age. And the younger dramatists could raise a protest too: the prologue to Brome's *The Court Beggar* (1632) asserts that here 'no gaudy Sceane Shall give instructions, what his plot doth meane', and Shirley in *Changes, or Love in a Maze* (1632) equates new masque with old jig, contemptuously levelling the tasteful Carolines with the rude Elizabethans:

> *Dan.* A masque will be delightful to the ladies.
> *Cap.* Oh, sir, what plays are taking without these
> Pretty devices? Many gentlemen
> Are not, as in the days of understanding,
> Now satisfied without a jig, which since
> They cannot, with their honour, call for after
> The play, they look to be serv'd up in the middle:
> Your dance is the best language of some comedies,
> And footing runs away with all; a scene
> Express'd with life of art, and squared to nature,
> Is dull and phlegmatic poetry.   (IV. ii.)

Most often these protests were mere registerings of discontent, for the playwrights knew well enough who gave the drama's laws.

Within the framework of the spectacle, the audience demanded a fanciful splendour, a romantic escape into a world where there were none of the threats that they themselves knew but instead elegant menaces that were foreign to them. And these escapes the dramatists gave in plenty: even the sober Massinger spent much of his time in fabricating remote tales, only recurring to the here and now when his critical spirit grew too strong for docile submission. Jonson's chorus before Act II of *The Magnetick Lady: or, Humors Reconcil'd* (1632) speaks as contemptuously as Sidney on the subject of rambling plays which trace the glorious career of the hero from infancy to empire: in the details of his charge he must be thinking

of the past, echoing his earlier complaint in the prologue
to *Every Man in his Humour* (1598), but his

> These miracles would please, I assure you: and take the
> *People!*

shows that he finds no real progression towards maturity.
Brome's prologue to *A Joviall Crew: Or, The Merry
Beggars* (1641) finds romantic adventures singularly inappropriate to 'these sad and tragick daies', but expresses
a willingness to conform to a practice which he thus
scornfully summarises:

> (Our Comick Writers finding that Romances
> Of Lovers, through much travell and distresse,
> Till it be thought, no Power can redresse
> Th' afflicted Wanderers, though stout Chevalry
> Lend all his aid for their delivery;
> Till, lastly, some impossibility
> Concludes all strife, and makes a Comedie).

But 'sad and tragick daies' have a habit of demanding
escapism in the drama.

When they were not demanding escape, the people of
this time could welcome a witty turn of speech, especially
if personal slander anointed the tip of the shaft. As early
as Chapman's *All Fools* (1604) we find a prologue protest-
ing against the personal application of a playwright's jests,
and two years later the epilogue to Marston's *The Wonder
of Women or The Tragedie of Sophonisba* insists that the
play is free from 'taxinges indiscreet'.[1] But the Caroline
playwrights, who generally echoed these protests, hint at
the extent of the practice through their very assertion of
innocence. There are, says Davenant in the prologue to

---

[1] Cf. the dedication to *Volpone* (1606) and the induction to *Bartholomew
Fair* (1614), where Jonson protests vigorously against searching for real-
life counterparts to characters seen in a play.

The Witts (1634), spectators who demand that the playwright's mirth should

> not at all
> Tickle, or stir their lungs, but shake their gall.

Ford's prologue to *The Broken Heart* (1629) avers that his
title lends no expectation of 'some lame jibe At place or
persons', and looks back to an imagined golden time when
'innocence and sweetness crowned' the poet's bays. And
the prologue, by the actor Theophilus Bird, to Ford's *The
Ladies Triall* (1638) finds both wit and its perversions a
sad falling-off:

> Wit, wit's the word in fashion, that alone
> Cries up the poet, which, though neatly shown,
> Is rather censur'd, oftentimes, than known.
>
> He who will venture on a jest, that can
> Rail on another's pain, or idly scan
> Affairs of state, O, he's the only man!
>
> A goodly approbation, which must bring
> Fame with contempt by such a deadly sting!
> The Muses chatter, who were wont to sing.
>
> Your favour in what we present to-day;
> Our fearless author boldly bids me say
> He tenders you no satire, but a play.

The reduction of the theatre from the grand, Gothick
proportions of forty years before could hardly have been
better conveyed than in this assertion that song had been
abandoned for chatter. But sometimes the dramatists
would defend themselves from the charge of personal
satire by urging that it was the spectators' fault if they
found themselves hit when a general folly was portrayed:
this is Shirley's defence in the prologue to *The Duke's
Mistris* (1636) and the argument that Massinger gives to

Paris in his magnificent plea for the stage in *The Roman Actor* (1626). Marmion, however, in the prologue to *A Fine Companion* (1633) claims that the dramatist has a right to brand the vices of particular men, though he himself will not make use of this.

But wit has another string to its bow, a string that the Caroline spectators liked to hear plucked—bawdry. Yet the playwrights are always avowing the chastity of their language, though often enough counterpoising this with the free lewdness of their plays. Shirley in *The Lady of Pleasure* (1635) satirically introduces a gallant as one who 'censures plays that are not bawdy' (I. i), and in the prologue to *The Coronation* he assures his spectators that

> there doth flow
> No under-mirth, such as doth lard the scene
> For coarse delight; the language here is clean.

As we have seen, this prologue goes on to invoke the ladies, who traditionally shrink from over-plain mirth. The prologue to his *The Doubtful Heir* (1640) gives the same assurance:

> you are
> So far from danger in this amorous war,
> Not the least rude uncivil language shall
> Approach your ear, or make one cheek look pale.

This play was acted in Dublin, and the prologue is that for the Dublin stage, so that we have interesting evidence from it that the London refinement had captured even the theatre of Shirley's exile. But indeed the bawdry of Caroline years was commonly less gross than that of preceding times: the very professional writer like Brome has rough horse-play in his action and grossness in his speech, but even he makes a disclaimer in the prologue to *The Weeding of the Covent-Garden. Or the Middlesex-Justice of Peace*

(1632). This is one of his most vigorous plays, yet he feels called on to assert that

> We shall present no Scandal or Abuse,
> To vertue or to honour.

This is at first sight surprising: we can understand Massinger in the prologue spoken at the court performance of *The Emperor of the East* (1631) boasting that the play contains nothing "But what the queen without a blush might hear", but Brome had neither Massinger's sobriety nor Davenant's skilful adaptation to circumstance. We must, in fact, see the franker coarseness of some Caroline plays arising partly from the playwright's own desire and partly from the influence of the still not despicable popular faction: the people of the court were not averse to moral grossness, but their taste in bawdry was too cultivated to welcome the easy verbal plainness of the earlier theatre. Certainly we cannot claim freedom from real grossness in many of the plays, but there is, in general, neither Elizabethan orotundity nor Restoration sharpness.

The newer dramatic style was not free from Elizabethan and Jacobean involutions—it could use 'conceits', and burlesque them, on occasion—but the trend was towards a plain dress for thought and feeling. Davenant and Massinger, even Shirley, we read with less care for the complexities of sound and sense than we give to their predecessors, and sometimes the desire for clarity of style is made articulate. The prologue to Shirley's *The Brothers* (1626) indicates the author's preference for plain language:

> He would have you believe no language good
> And artful, but what's clearly understood; ...
> He says the times are dangerous; who knows
> What treason may be wrapt in giant prose,
> Or swelling verse, at least to sense?

And Alexander Brome, writing commendatory verses for Richard Brome's plays when they were printed in 1653, finds his plainness of style especially laudable:

> No stradling Tetrasyllables are brought
> To fill up room, and little spell, or nought.
> No Bumbast Raptures, and no lines immense,
> That's call'd (by th' curtesie of *England*) sence.
> But all's so plaine, that one may see, he made it
> T' inform the understanding, not invade it.

This development is not at all surprising in view of the palates that the playwrights had in mind: spectacle, romance, the easy wit of slander or ribaldry were the dishes that most pleased, and the way of serving them had to be efficient, untroublesome to the jaded guest. Much criticism of pre-Civil War drama has overstressed the languor of these years: it was, after all, a period that allowed Ford to flourish, and gave Davenant, Shirley and Brome an atmosphere in which they could grow to whatever heights of wit, strength and comic force their own natures allowed them; it did produce a masterpiece in *'Tis Pity She's a Whore*, and numerous works of talent such as *A Joviall Crew*, *The Platonic Lovers*, *The Roman Actor*, *The Cardinal* and *The Witty Fair One*; its general level of attainment was even in many respects higher than that of the early Restoration years. Yet the palates of the audience were sick, like those of London audiences between the two World Wars. Difficulty was estranging, and the easy thrill or laugh was trebly welcome: the more searching study was eschewed for the light relief of a vicarious existence.

Plays of different types could win popularity from their refined audience, but nearly always the characteristic indispensable for success was some measure of withdrawal from the actual. The dramatists of the time were often inclined to comment on state affairs, to express their growing scepticism of the postulates they had inherited,[1] but these things are incidental in their plays. Walter Montague and Queen Henrietta, as author and chief actress, wearied the court with *The Shepherd's Paradise* (1633), but the play had doubtless won the liking of the influential queen because of its remoteness from actuality, its pseudo-Platonic ramblings on love, its absurd disregard of the non-genteel. The court liked *Florimène* (1635) better, for that entertained with spectacle and dance, and could even derive 'a great deal of content'[2] from George Wilde's *Loves Hospitall* (1636), which exploited the comedy of the blind, the deaf, the dumb and the lame: pastoral or comical might please, so long as the contact with the actual was of the most fleeting. Wilde's play was at least unpretentious, and would go well enough on the stage for an audience not inclined to be squeamish with pity and delighting in a semi-abstract stage-fun. Shirley, with none of Wilde's clumsiness, achieves a similar puppet-show effect in *Changes, or Love in a Maze* (1632). When confronted with the success or failure of a play in the Caroline period, we must remember this tendency to abstraction. Doubtless it was what made Jonson's last plays so ill-received, what roused his fury at their reception: he could be abstract in method, but his persistent contact with the actual jarred upon current susceptibilities.

When plays of earlier years were revived, the prologues and epilogues often expressed doubt as to the reception the new audience would give them. One prologue[3] used for Caroline revivals of Fletcher's *Thierry and Theodoret*

---

[1] Cf. " Pacifism in Caroline Drama", *The Durham University Journal*, March, 1939, for comment on their growing doubt of military 'honour' and patriotism.

[2] Anthony Wood, quoted by Alfred Harbage, *Cavalier Drama*, p. 141.

[3] We can date it *c.* 1636, as the revived play is said to have been in fashion 'some twenty yeares agoe': this could not be true of *The Noble Gentleman*, so we must assume that the prologue was originally written for the revival of *Thierry and Theodoret*.

(1616) and his *The Noble Gentleman* (1626) begins by exclaiming at the uncertainty of public taste:

> Wit is become an Antick; and puts on
> As many shapes of variation,
> To court the times applause, as the times dare
> Change severall fashions; nothing is thought rare
> Which is not new and follow'd.

Similarly, a Caroline epilogue used for revivals of Beaumont's *The Woman-Hater* (1606) and Fletcher's *The Noble Gentleman* apologetically describes each play as 'this old monument of wit'.

Heywood, in his prologue to *A Challenge for Beavtie* (1635), claims that English drama has risen far superior to that of Italy or France or Spain or the Netherlands, but laments that now the playwrights imitate their inferiors, forget the lofty subjects of earlier years and write only of 'puling Lovers, craftie Bawdes or cheates'. And Shirley prefixes to his tired and creaking neo-miracle *St. Patrick for Ireland* (1637) a prologue which utters the whole and unpleasing truth about his audience: their sick palates are not even consistent in their longings, and the playwright is distressed that so much labour must go into a play when it is so hastily swallowed and often regurgitated:

> We know not what will take; your palates are
> Various, and many of them sick, I fear:
> We can but serve up what our poets dress;
> And not considering cost, or pains to please,
> We should be very happy if, at last,
> We could find out the humour of your taste,
> That we might fit, and feast it, so that you
> Were constant to yourselves, and kept that true;
> For some have their opinions so diseas'd,
> They come not with a purpose to be pleas'd:
> Or, like some birds that leave the flow'ry fields,
> They only stoop at that corruption yields. . . .

would each soul were masculine!
For your own sakes, we wish all here to-day
Knew but the art and labour of a play;
Then you would value the true muses' pain,
The throes and travail of a teeming brain.[1]

The weariness of the fickle public taste, of not knowing what may be the next fashion, is not of course individual to Caroline dramatists: it is reflected often enough in other times and places—in Calderón's *The Devotion of the Cross* there is a poet who despairs of pleasing tastes so diverse as those of clerk and clown and resents that they must be his judges—but the playwrights of this time had special cause for finding the state of affairs irksome. They were not, as a whole, men who were content to write for themselves, depending on their public for things which they themselves hardly realised, but were essentially purveyors of goods to a difficult market. Often, as notably in Massinger, they would discipline their natural bent of mind, torment it into the fashionable curve, but the continual modifications of this curve made them at times almost lose heart.

This, then, is a picture of the public they addressed, this is what explains their 'tone'. Even Ford, the most independent as well as the finest of the company, inevitably reflects his climate. Theophilus Bird, in the prologue to *The Ladies Triall*, observed that the Muses were now chattering, and it was a new language for them. They were to learn how chatter could be made into a dramatic vehicle, and then they might speak through Wycherley and Congreve, but the immediate inheritors of the Elizabethan tradition found themselves speaking a strange tongue. Speak it they had to, for it was their audience's, but the syntax was uncomfortably novel and the accidence often politely gross.

---

[1] Jonson had uttered much the same complaint in his prologue to *The New Inn; or, The Light Heart* (1629).

Chapter 9

LOVE AS A DRAMATIC THEME

IT is no longer believed that Restoration drama was a new invention, or a derivative from France, shut off by an eighteen years' silence from the drama of 1642. The links between Restoration and Caroline drama are, in fact, now easily recognised by those who look for them, and kinship is seen between Etherege and Shirley, between Dryden and Davenant. But our terminology often suggests the older, outmoded view: we may speak of 'Elizabethan' drama when we wish to refer to any drama from Elizabeth's accession to the Civil War, as if the whole period were homogeneous and uniformly differentiated from the 'Restoration' drama that followed. A more exact use of the term 'Elizabethan' and a more frequent distinction between 'Jacobean' and 'Caroline' would reflect more accurately the true state of things, and would more easily lead us to recognise that the plays of the years just before 1642 are nearer in form and spirit to Restoration comedies and tragedies than they are to the plays of Shakespeare's time.

In comedy, the path from *Gammer Gurton* to *Sir Fopling Flutter* is one of easy gradation, for the canvas is gradually restricted, the social tone gradually elevated, the language gradually refined, the comic view of the human animal gradually more exquisitely perceived. Though individual dramatists make their various departures from the norm, the process of change is steadily carried through. But in tragedy there is a marked change which becomes apparent from the early years of the seventeenth century: up till then, we may call 'Elizabethan' tragedy a drama of

182

power; after that, it became a drama of sex. One has only to glance at the titles of plays before and after 1600 to see how the later drama was preoccupied with women and love. Shakespeare and Chapman belong chiefly to the earlier school, for in them sex exists either as simply part of human experience, which the dramatist's eye lights upon almost by chance, or as simply the occasion of a tragic happening: Chapman writes of love in *Bussy D'Ambois* and Shakespeare makes a play out of jealousy in *Othello*, but Bussy is more than a lover and Othello's disaster is not merely the loss of a wife. *Troilus and Cressida* and *Antony and Cleopatra* mark a point of transition, being studies in the interrelations of sex and power.

Seventeenth-century drama is, in fact, hag-ridden by sex. Even when the subject of a play is remote from human love, as in Massinger and Dekker's *The Virgin Martyr* (1620) or Shirley's *St. Patrick for Ireland* (1637), the dramatist's obsession soon makes itself apparent. Massinger and Dekker see Dorothea with a repressed sensuality, and extract a thrill from her martyrdom; Shirley makes the background of his St. Patrick story a tissue of love-intrigues. And the increasing salaciousness of comedy comes from the same source as the tragic writers' obsession: the coarse humours of a Gammer Gurton or a Falstaff are exchanged for the thrill of vicarious sensuality. All through the seventeenth century, the drama reflects a relaxation from action and a withdrawal into contemplation; and the spectacle contemplated is set in motion not by the desire for aggrandisement but by the desire for sensual satisfaction. 'Ambition' and 'revenge' remain, indeed, as stock dramatic motives, but they are not very much believed in. Vindice finds his mistress again in the blood he sheds, and Ferdinand of Calabria aches for the Duchess, his sister, whom he kills.

This turning away from the contemplation of other

183

human characteristics in order to dissect the heart of a
lover is of considerable interest to us, with our modern
theatres so generally concerned with love-relationships.
Mr. F. L. Lucas has sought to excuse this narrowing of
interest:

> It is well that literature should turn to harp on other heart-
> strings when it can; but it is well also to recognise that for our
> world love remains the great source of real tragedy. In a peaceful
> civilisation it must be so; in wilder ages when life itself is in
> perpetual danger, men feel more strongly about other things.
> "Love does not vex the man that begs his bread," says a shrewd
> fragment of Euripides.[1]

But this shows an over-anxiety to excuse and justify,
for the drama of sex is, fortunately, not always with us:
man in his relation to God and man in his relation to
society are the dramatist's concern as well as man in his
relation to woman. The problem of war is part of the problem of man and society, and it engaged the minds of
dramatists before and around 1600; the problem of man
and God was explored by the Greeks, by medieval writers,
by Shakespeare and some not insignificant moderns.
Nevertheless, to consider man in the whole context of his
existence requires either a stout faith or a stouter courage,
and most playwrights narrow their attention to sex when
they have lost interest in the problems of society.

Not that society failed to interest the early seventeenth
century. The plays of the time are full of comments and
strictures on man's behaviour to man, on the organisation
of government, on the rights and duties of kingship.[2] But
the circumstances were such, and the mentality of the
dramatists was such, that these comments and strictures
were rarely more than incidental. It was from outside the

---

[1] *Tragedy in Relation to Aristotle's Poetics*, p. 103.
[2] For dramatic comments on war, cf. "Pacifism in Caroline Drama",
The Durham University Journal, March, 1939.

theatrical sphere that the challenge came to kingly power in the mid-century, and we get only occasional premonitions in the plays. The dramatists in general reposed on the existing social order, girding a little at its unevennesses but with little thought for a change of pillow. Seventeenth-century drama is a drama of peace, and thus almost inevitably a drama of sex.

Therein lies its great weakness. Any dramatist who documents phenomena of only one kind, whose attentions are dragged only one way, can very easily make his play a mere dream-fulfilment of his desires. The theistic dramatist makes God again in his own image, the social dramatist sees quick triumph for his panacea, the sex-dramatist delights in the mere externalising of his lusts. These traps can be avoided, but they are always near for playwrights whose gaze is fixed. Middleton and Tourneur, as well as Ford, impress us with the tremendous power of their human revelation, but their plays are disordered, not only superficially in structure, but profoundly in idea: the life of the tragic hero is restricted to a sex-life, the thought of the play is largely restricted to thought about sex. They cannot be justified as unconsciously anticipating Freud: for them the whole of life was not governed by sex, and they turned away wilfully from the whole to a part. Their very genius makes the narrowing of view the more regrettable.

The comic dramatist, because he is generally further from his human material, does not suffer to the same extent from this restriction of vision. Since his aim is to expose human littleness, it matters little whether the braggart soldier or the incompetent keeper is his victim. But comedy at its deepest level comes near to tragedy in its sympathy with the persons of the drama, and then the dramatist's vision must be wide if his play is to have a more than sporadic validity. That is why *The Plain*

Dealer fails so badly and why *The Way of the World*
stands so triumphantly above the other plays of its time:
Wycherley could not relate his hatred for the Olivias of
the world to any scheme of living; Congreve directs the
whole of his comic writing to an elucidation of the
importance of love. Mirabel and Millamant are no more
only people in love than Chehov's Three Sisters are. On
the other hand, *The Country Wife* and many lesser plays
of the seventeenth century are great successes, for there
the comedy makes no attempt to go deep, is content with
exposing folly and with assuming the background of the
writer's normality. Only when normality is explored does
comedy achieve the status of tragedy.[1]

The one important difference between the drama
immediately before 1642 and the drama after 1660—
beyond the very material fact that Charles I's reign had
neither a Congreve nor a Wycherley—is that tragedy
proper disappeared in the Restoration. Its place was taken
first by the heroic play, in which an idealised love and
honour became the sole motivating forces in the hero's
character, so that there was little connection between the
protagonist and human nature and the play was an
eccentric example of a wish-fulfilment, and then by the
pathetic play, in which the sensitive nerves of the dramatist
were imparted to the spectators without any purpose
beyond that of conveying the delights of sensitivity.
Tourneur communicates an experience, narrow and un-
related to the whole of his experience; Dryden plays with
nostalgic fancies; Otway begs us to smoke hashish with
him. This tendency to escape from the drama of sex to an
idealised view of love-relations is a natural reaction, and it
shows itself, though sometimes in a form rather different

[1] The exploration of normality may be indirect, through the drawing
of gigantic caricatures suggestive of human potentialities, as in Falstaff and
Volpone.

from the Restoration heroic drama, just as clearly in pre-1642 plays. The man who is hag-ridden will often strive to pretend that an angel rides him.

By analysing the situation in pre-1642 drama, we can see how close is the link with the Restoration. After 1660 the atmosphere is a little more rarified, for the narrowing of the audience reached the point where the drama became the utterance of a single class, and the post-War and post-Interregnum reactions accentuated the concern with the delights and torments of peace, but in spirit there is little difference between Shadwell and Brome, between Aphra Behn and Shirley—except that Brome and Shirley are much more skilled in their witty depiction of human littleness. In recent years Restoration comedy has been overpraised, for it has been read under the shadow of Congreve: actually it is much closer to pre-1642 plays in its surface-merriment and its occasional fumblings into the depths than it is to *The Way of the World*, a mature and assured play. The main purpose of this chapter is to show how Caroline and Restoration playwrights resemble each other in their ways of escape from sex-obsession.

The sex-obsession rises, of course, from the very withdrawal from extra-sexual action, and at the same time may carry over into the depiction of sex-experience the exuberance which was manifested earlier in the plays of power. Ford's *'Tis Pity She's a Whore* (1627) demonstrates exactly this, as Tourneur's plays had done. But often the vein of sensuality runs thin, so that one gets this over-precious kind of writing in Shackerley Marmion's *The Antiquary* (1635), where the piquancy of the words is heightened in that they are spoken by a woman to another woman disguised as a page:

> Do but yield unto me,
> My arms shall be thy sphere to wander in,
> Circled about with spells to charm these fears;

And, when thou sleep'st, Cupid shall crown thy slumbers
With thousand shapes of lustful dalliance:
Then will I bathe thee in ambrosia,
And from my lips distil such nectar on thee,
Shall make thy flesh immortal.   (IV. i.)

It is not surprising that such things palled, that in violent withdrawal the playwright often inveighs against womankind. This he does with increasing frequency from the beginning of the century: Beaumont and Fletcher minister nicely to the taste for abuse, and their successors regularly depict heroes turning against heroines, not with the dumb astonishment of a misunderstood lover but with the fierce repulsion of a sated debauchee. Thus Cowley's Truman in *The Guardian* (1642):

What are these women made of? Sure we men
Are of some better mold. Their vows and oaths
Are like the poisonous Spiders subtil net,
As dangerous to entrap, and broke as soon.
Their love, their faith, their selves enslav'd to passion.
Nothing's at their command, except their tears,
And we frail men, whom such heat-drops entice.

(III. iii.)

Women are pretentious and venal, lecherous and inconstant, is the continual refrain. And there is a touch of hatred in these lines from Davenant's *The Witts* (1634), where proleptically we meet the Restoration fine lady, coarsely brandishing her refinement:

I would kiss thee, Engine, but for an odd
Nice humour in my lips; they blister at
Inferior breath.   (II. i.)

If woman is at whiles hated, it is for the love which holds man to her. It is a slavery, an abnegation of man's superiority, his independence, his reason. Marston had many an utterance where male anger at this state of things is conveyed, and Fletcher knew how to exploit the vein. In Henry Glapthorne's *The Tragedy of Albertus Wallenstein* (1634) the young Albertus finds love opposed to reason (for the thing loved so easily becomes loathsome) and to the soul (for love is fleshly and sordid), but he is soon again entrapped when his Isabella comes to him. Massinger, too, more deliberate, more master of himself than most of his contemporaries, found his feelings rise against love's dominion. Particularly was he revolted by uxoriousness, which he shows as degradation in *The Duke of Milan* (1621) and *The Emperor of the East* (1631).

In general, however, the reaction from sensuality to perverted puritanism is not so marked in the Caroline years as earlier. The ways of escape for the contemporaries of Ford were generally three in number: (1) into attacks on marriage, with a retention of libertinism, free and untroubled (the way of Restoration comedy); (2) into the modish praise of Platonic Love, for which Henrietta Maria was partly responsible; (3) into the fanciful world where idealised love and idealised honour were seen as conflicting, with love a little less ideal than honour (the way of the Restoration heroic play). The first way appears realistic, derived directly from the playwright's experience; the second and third are more obviously 'escapist', coming from a turning of the back upon the actual. Platonic Love was a passing fashion, ridiculed even while it flourished, but the other ways endured not only into the Restoration period but far into the succeeding years. Not one of the three ways is new, for all are to be found in the plays around 1600, the first in Marston, the second in Chapman's *Monsieur D'Olive*, and the third sporadically in Fletcher. But the Caroline plays continue the first, and develop the second and third.

We must now follow the Caroline playwrights down

each of these ways of escape, noting in turn how each way is pursued without plan, without faith, but with a desire to find relief from the sex-obsession. The study will not, perhaps, raise Caroline plays in the reader's estimation, but it at least provides an object-lesson on the dangers of one-angled drama.

Marriage, the playwrights tell us, dulls the appetite. Brome in *The City Wit, or, The Woman wears the Breeches* (1628) puts it in this way:

> *Cra.* . . . you have a Wife Sir.
> *Tic.* Pish, who cares to drink out of a River? What I can command out of duty hath but a dull relish. Had not *Danae* been kept in her brass Tower, she had never tempted a Gods piercing.   (IV. i.)

And the same man's *The Queen and Concubine* (1635), a prolonged tragicomedy which shows how Heaven is on the side of suffering virtue, speaks with the playwright's own tongue when scolding and cuckoldry are weighed against each other:

> His 'tother wife would not have us'd him thus.
> Quiet Cuckoldrie is better then scolding chastitie all
>   the world over.   (IV. vii.)

Cowley makes his Aurelia in *The Guardian* (1642) imagine the fine lady's life she will lead in marriage, a life given up to dress and vanity, in which her husband is valued only for his wealth and his knighthood. Shackerley Marmion in *Hollands Leaguer* (1631) cynically gives advice on how a woman may tyrannise over her husband: she shall use him as a shelter for her reputation, send him on foot while she rides in her coach, and make him pay dearly for every privilege. This girding at male subjection becomes more explicit when the rake Fowler inveighs against marriage in Shirley's *The Witty Fair One* (1628), though later he is converted from his prejudice, and won in marriage by his Penelope. So, too, even in the tragedy *Love's Crueltie* (1631) Shirley makes Hippolito rail against marriage like any Restoration rake, avowing that wedlock shall not ensnare him till the ripe age of one-and-thirty. So Androlio in Davenant's *The Distresses* (1639) speaks, when the seduced Amiana tries to persuade him to matrimony. For marriage, we are told in the same play, is a man's penalty for making love:

> marriage is a kind of foolish penance we
> Are often put unto, for wasting thus
> Our precious time in making silly love. (IV. v.)

But the complaints are not given to men alone. The dramatists could be sufficiently detached in their repugnance to see that it might be shared. As early as 1603 Crispinella in *The Dutch Courtezan* attacked the tyranny and general unpleasantness of husbands; in 1610 Tamyra in *The Revenge of Bussy D'Ambois* protested against the dependence of wives; and Fletcher's *The Honest Man's Fortune* (1613) and *The Knight of Malta* (1618) make women echo these complaints.[1] Shirley makes Mistress Carol in *Hide Park* (1632) compare at length the pleasures of single life with the vexations of marriage; and Lady Yellow in Glapthorne's *The Hollander* (1636) speaks of "the obedient slavery, due to marriage". In fact, the complaints from both wives and husbands are led to their natural climax in Shirley's *The Gamester* (1633):

> I would there were a parson to unmarry us!
> If any of our clergy had that faculty,
> He might repair the old, and build as many
> New abbeys through the kingdom in a twelvemonth.
>
> (I. i.)

---

[1] The passage spoken by a 'Gentlewoman' in *The Knight of Malta*, I. ii, seems to echo Tamyra verbally.

These complaints, of course, are facetious, and are almost uniformly followed by an acceptance of the married state. But they stand clearly for a realistic appraisal of marriage, with a lifting of its romantic cloak. They provide the raw material for a mature critical comedy, but the dramatists rarely achieve that. Brome might have been capable of it, but his delight in horse-play was too strong for him to produce thoughtful drama in this kind; Davenant touches it in *News from Plymouth* (1635) and *The Witts* (1634), but his touch is often fumbling and his wit insufficiently keen; Shirley in *The Witty Fair One* (1628) comes indeed close, but his aim is uncertain. Instead of achieving the good critical comedy to which their inclinations often led them, they hesitate from extending to a whole play the attitude of mind which so often rings true in occasional passages. They are potentially capable of *The Beaux' Stratagem* or the comic scenes of *Marriage à la Mode*, but they did not often care to make the attempt. They wished to escape from the problem of marriage, not to face it.

Yet their minds were exercised over marriage, and often in their plays we get a casual anticipation of Congreve's seriousness. Sex-equality is then implicit. The wit-combats of hero and heroine, prominent from the last decade of the sixteenth century, occupy a key-position in the economy of the play, and are made to conform to the newer naturalistic tone.

The Witty Fair One is typical of this kind of play. Like most Restoration comedies, it loses itself in intrigue, the language gives pleasure without sparkle, and the characters are taken from the usual dramatic store. It is not surprising that Downes tells us it was popular on the Restoration stage, for it was thoroughly in the post-1660 mode. The only complaint one can raise is that it does not take itself seriously: the puppets are made to go through their motions, and the showman's concern is to startle us by the skill of his wire-pulling. The same objection can, in general, be brought against Restoration comedy, but the commonness of the charge does not invalidate it.

Actually Beaumont and Fletcher might have produced the frank sex-comedy that the age demanded, if only they had not been concerned with supplying so many of the age's demands. *The Wild Goose Chase* is well known for its anticipation of *Man and Superman*, but its treatment is most unshavian, almost tearful in some of the Oriana scenes. But in *The Womans Prize, or The Tamer Tam'd* (1606) Beaumont used *The Taming of the Shrew* and the *Lysistrata* as bases for a lively sketch:

Petruchio has married Maria. His first wife was a shrew, and he had mastered her. But Maria, with the aid of her cousin Biancha, keeps him at a distance. He gives in to her conditions, but she continues to plague him: he cannot approach her, she wastes his substance, she has him shut up as plague-stricken when he pretends illness to soften her, she welcomes the project when he says he will go abroad, she affects relief when he is brought in apparently dead. But then she relents, considering that his lesson has been learned.

The tricks of Maria grow wearisome. At first, the state of siege, in which she and Biancha are joined by City and Country Wives, is an interesting echo of the *Lysistrata*, a mass-revolt against the masculine system of things, but after the first two acts her devices are not particularly comic in themselves and weary in the accumulation. But, though the play is mediocre, it is notable among the sex-comedies of the time: the war is open, and its unsubtle violence does not disguise its trend of feeling. The epilogue, in fact, takes its stand on sex-equality:

> The Tamer's tam'd, but so, as nor the men
> Can find one just cause to complain of, when

They fitly do consider in their lives,
  They should not reign as Tyrants o'er their wives.
Nor can the Women from this president
  Insult, or triumph; it being aptly meant,
To teach both Sexes due equality;
  And as they stand bound, to love mutually.

Neither Fletcher nor his successors followed the hint of *The Woman's Prize*, and *The Witty Fair One* remains the type of Caroline critical comedy. Yet it is worth noting that several of the plays of the time have bargaining-scenes, anticipatory of *The Way of the World*, where man or woman brings a list of conditions to be agreed to before marriage. Thus in Marmion's *A Fine Companion* (1633) Dotario is so terrified by Aemilia's threats of her behaviour after marriage that he comes armed with a string of provisos. Massinger's *The City Madam* (1632) makes both Anne and Mary lay down conditions, Anne being particularly Restoration in her bargaining: after requiring her 'will in all things whatsoever', she demands all the panoply of fashion and concludes almost in Millamant's terms:

These toys subscribed to,
And you continuing an obedient husband,
Upon all fit occasions you shall find me
A most indulgent wife. (II. ii.)

In Shirley's *Hide Park* Fairfield asks Mistress Carol to swear to something he will propose to her, giving her the opportunity to make all the exceptions she pleases, provided that she makes them in advance. Her list of exceptions is very like a list of marriage-conditions. Glapthorne's *Wit in a Constable* (1639) has two such bargaining-scenes: in the first, Valentine tries to ensure his after-marriage state by demanding that Grace shall prove obedient, shall be willing to entertain his friends, and shall never lament her choice of a husband; in the second, Clare and Grace mockingly lay down their terms to Hold-fast and Timothy. All these scenes are engaging, and often the wit is keen, but our reaction to them is rarely more than a recognition that the year 1700 and *The Way of the World* are approaching. These plays hardly exist for us in their own right, but only as an anticipation of something else. It was easier to abuse marriage and delineate the joys of libertinism than to explore the comedy of normal life. Most of the witty jesting on marriage in the seventeenth century represents an escape from actuality through bawdry.

Platonic Love appears occasionally in the drama soon after 1600. There it seems odd, incongruous with the still vigorous humours of the stage. Perhaps it survives as a legacy from Spenser, but it is often a holy passion outside marriage and subsisting on incorporeal delight. Thus in Chapman's *Monsieur D'Olive* (1604) Vandome has a Platonic mistress Marcellina, and her husband is made to regret that he has thought the worse of her for that: it is true that other characters in the play suspect that these Neo-Platonics are a convenient veil for an actual intrigue, but the plot gives no justification to their suspicions. Then in Fletcher's *The Knight of Malta* (1618) the married Oriana cools Miranda's passion by discoursing to him of Platonic affection: there is more than a trace of snobbery in her words, and the whole passage contrasts quaintly with Fletcher's delighted portrayal of lust elsewhere in the play. The idea, however, was more than a dramatic cliché which a Fletcher could use, for it finds its best utterance in the words of Clermont, Chapman's most thoughtful hero, in *The Revenge of Bussy D'Ambois* (1610). His love is reasoning, Platonic, and masculine, and his rejection of passion has all the intellectual puritanism of a passionately thinking Elizabethan. In him the recoil from love's trap has dignity.

195

Jonson in *The New Inn, or The Light Heart* (1629) is orthodox rather than fashionable in his Platonism. His hero Lovel undertakes to give two addresses to his mistress Frances, on Love and Valour respectively. For Love he refers to the *Symposium,* for Valour he demands intelligence: both speeches are finely wrought, deliberate pieces of writing, and the discourse on Love is admirably counterpointed by Latimer's wooing of Frank, a girl disguised as a boy disguised as a girl. This is indeed far from the crude and fashionable snobbery of *The Knight of Malta*: Jonson's Lovel no more denies the physical than Spenser does, nor does he stand aside from common things like the quite exceptional Clermont: his concern is only to see the physical as an image of the spiritual.

Dr. Tillyard has commented that the Elizabethan would feel little discomfort 'if a man was both far advanced in the process of Platonic love and at the same time satisfied the simple craving of the senses in a simple way: provided of course the persons concerned were kept rigidly distinct'.[1] This ambivalent attitude can be seen persisting in Chapman and, less surely, in Jonson, but for Fletcher and his followers the contradiction becomes more explicit and the writer's sincerity much more questionable. Encouraged by the taste of the Queen, which manifested itself in court masque and play, the typical Caroline dramatist paid lip-service to the prevailing mode. Thus in Marmion's *Hollands Leagver* the heroine Faustina keeps the amorous Philautus at bay by denying the name of love to that which is 'conversant in beastly appetites' (III. iv). We are reminded that Marmion wrote a *Cupid and Psyche*, a poem in which he saw the love of those immortals as an allegory of the soul. So Glapthorne in *Albertus Wallenstein* makes Frederick protest to Emilia that his love is ultimately for her excellent mind:

[1] *Five Poems 1470–1870*, 1948, p. 46.

I love your minde,
Your excellent minde, and for its sake, the pure
Shrine, which containes that blessing, this fair building,
This pallace of all happinesse, and intreat you,
As you have mercy in you, to take pitty
Upon my loves stern sufferings, and redresse them,
By your consent to take me for your husband.   (II. ii.)

Consciously or unconsciously, the dramatists did this
sort of thing with a twisted tongue, and their laughter at
their own escape is often merry. Glapthorne, for example,
burlesques the fashion in *The Hollander* (1636). There
Popinjay wooes Dalinea: she is delighted to receive his
suit, but affects a Platonic shrinking: he assures her of his
love's idealism, using the words that Glapthorne had
given seriously to Frederick in *Albertus Wallenstein*.

Shirley has a malicious stroke in *The Duke's Mistris*
(1636). His Horatio has a humorous passion for ugly
women, thinking they are more likely to be faithful, and
he ironically explains his humour thus:

To be short, ladies,
Howe'er you may interpret it my humour,
Mine's a Platonic love; give me the soul,
I care not what coarse flesh and blood enshrine it;
Preserve your beauties, this will fear no blasting.   (III. ii.)

The ugly Fiametta to whom he is paying his addresses is
quite enough to blast the modish pretence of superfine
spirituality.

But one play is almost wholly devoted to a burlesque of
the fashion. Davenant's prologue to *The Platonic Lovers*
(1635) refers to his subject as one given by the Court and
perhaps incomprehensible to the town. Unfortunately he
does not confine himself to this subject: doubtless to
please the town, he introduces a feeble villain Fredeline
whose machinations blunt the satire's edge. Even so, the
play should be better known as containing some of the

best topical satire of Caroline years. Its story runs as follows:

The Duke Theander is platonically in love with Eurithea, sister of Phylomont, a neighbouring Duke, who loves Theander's sister Ariola in the normal way. Theander will not consent to Ariola's marriage, for marriage is to him low and coarse. But his subjects wish him to marry and therefore administer an aphrodisiac: soon he is married to Eurithea, but she will agree to only Platonic raptures. Phylomont now has Theander's permission to marry Ariola, but meanwhile she has been converted to Platonism. The villainies of Fredeline, who has designs on Eurithea, are then set at work, and when these are defeated the four lovers decide it is better to live in the normal way.

In II. iii, we are given Platonic rhapsodies at length. Theander visits the sleeping Eurithea, and their conversation when she wakes has mocking echoes of *Romeo and Juliet*. Later the very name of Platonic Love is attacked, and the suggestion is made that Plato is an unsuitable godfather for the fashion. In II. v, Phylomont asks Theander for Ariola's hand: Theander is shocked by the grossness of the idea, and bids them 'beget reflections in each others' eyes'.

Before the end of the play the villainous Fredeline suggests that the Platonic fashion can be merely a cloak for infidelity. This, however, is an exceptional thrust, incongruous with the practice of Theander and Eurithea. The play as a whole ridicules the courtly way of escape as an unnatural folly. Davenant realises the snobbery of it, the implicit suggestion that fine people are of different stuff from the common. This snobbery was enduring, so that in 1658 Cowley's hero Truman in *The Cutter of Coleman-Street* thinks that love can exist only for the high-born:

Would I had been born some wretched Peasant's son,
And never known what Love or Riches were. (IV. iv.)

In fact, such snobbery has lasted longer than the seventeenth century, which was peculiar only in the eccentric form of its complacent fancy.

The third of the three ways of escape was pursued far less assiduously than either of the other two. It is the one that was to achieve full growth from *The Siege of Rhodes* (1656), and in Caroline years hesitation lies about it in its infancy. The plays of the time could glance cynically at 'honour',[1] so that even from its very beginnings this method of escape was one that commanded little belief.

A love-and-honour conflict is manifest in Fletcher's *The Island Princess* (1621). Armusia, a valiant Portuguese, wins the right to marry Quisara, sister of the King of Sidore. She had offered her hand to whoever should rescue her brother from captivity, for she expected her lover Dias to do this. But Armusia wins her love and, after she has attempted to make him change his faith, he is so eloquent that she turns Christian.

The conversion-motive here rings false—Fletcher has no scruples in juxtaposing conversion with bawdy talk, and Quisara's change of faith is poorly motivated—but it provided the setting for a love-and-honour conflict in Armusia. He has to choose between his love and his honour as a Portuguese gentleman, for his religion seems precisely that, just as Dias earlier in the play had to make the same choice when Quisara wished him to kill Armusia.

---

[1] Cf. "Pacifism in Caroline Drama", *loc. cit.* Even in seventeenth-century Spanish drama a protest against 'honour' can on occasion be raised. Calderón's *The Painter of Dishonour* and *The Devotion of the Cross* have husbands in them who bewail the necessity of preserving their marital honour: they have no love for their ruling code.

The play is well summarised when Pyniero, the virtuous nephew of Dias, remarks:

> These winds of love and honor, blow at all ends.   (III. i.)

Like Restoration heroic figures, Dias and Armusia exist as compounded of two impulses, which may be at odds: both are to be highly esteemed, but 'honour' must govern 'love'.

The same idea becomes explicit for a moment in Heywood's *A Challenge for Beavtie* (1635). The Spanish Valadaura has freed the English Ferrers from captivity: both love Petrocella, and when Valadaura bids Ferrers win the lady for him, Ferrers acknowledges the conflict within himself but has no doubt where his duty lies:

> Doubly captived:
> Honour should still preseede love: Sir, I will,
> Though I to cure another, my selfe kill.   (III. i.)

'Honour' appears neither as religion nor as friendship and gratitude in Davenant's *The Siege* (1629):[1] here it is military honour and loyalty to one's prince. The forces of Florence are besieging Pisa, and the Florentine Florello loves Bertolina, daughter of Pisa's Governor. He deserts and gets to her, but she is horrified and sends him back. Ultimately he finds it possible to retain his honour and win his love. The dialogue between them in III. iv shows Florello in Almanzor's toils, and Bertolina as Almahide, that voice of conscience.

The flatulent tempests of the heroic play come nearer their full frenzy in Shirley's *The Young Admirall* (1633). Here Vittori has to choose between giving his love

---

[1] The play was not published till 1673: it has been identified with *The Colonel*, licensed in 1629, but none of its major characters is a colonel. It may well have been written much later, and perhaps in part is even post-1660.

Cassandra up to death and betraying his country: she is
willing to die, but for him love is stronger than honour :

> *Vit.* I am in a tempest,
> And know not how to steer; destruction dwells
> On both sides.
>   *Cas.* Come, resolve.
>   *Vit.* I must—to let
> Thee live.—I will take arms;—forgive me then,
> Great Genius of my country, that, to save
> Her life, I bring my honour to the grave.   (III. i.)

Striking heroics appear before this, when Vittori shows
his love by the valour with which he defends his lady and
by his maudlin veneration of her: in II. ii a conversation
between the King of Sicily and the lady Rosinda is
interrupted by this stage-direction:

> *Enter Soldiers, pursued by* VITTORI *with his sword drawn,
> bearing* CASSANDRA, *insensible.* ·

After a little, Vittori grows furious:

> *K. of S.* Do you delight in wounds? resign that lady.
>   *Vit.*   Not while my hand can manage this; the blood
> You take, will make us walk on even pace
> To death, and when my soul can stay no longer,
> I'll leave a curse to blast you;

and concludes the scene with fantastic devotion:

> Oh my Cassandra,
> When at the expense of all my blood, I have bought
> Thy precious life from these hard-hearted men,
> Shed one tear on me, and I am paid agen.

This is ridiculous to us, but it was not to Sir Henry
Herbert, whose dramatic records contain a remarkable
encomium on the play: he found it a 'beneficial and

cleanly way of poetry' and hoped that both Shirley and other poets would continue in the vein.[1] It was a way of writing that could please a time so passionately desirous to find an object of veneration. Increasing scepticism, increasing repulsion from sexual tyranny, increasing doubt of the standards which were assumed to distinguish good conduct from bad—these led to a very exaltation of the things that were actually in question. Even the praise of the single life, of libertinism, has something nostalgic in it, as if the dramatists were anxious to convince themselves of their practical wisdom. And all this is equally true of Caroline and Restoration drama. The comic style changed to some extent after 1660—settings became more familiar, prose usurped the place of verse, licence of action was more noticeable—but the dilemma remained the same.

Thus each of the three ways of escape from the seventeenth-century preoccupation with sex brings with it its own reaction. The praise of libertinism is balanced by the fugitive and insubstantial attempts to look marriage squarely in the face; Neo-Platonism finds its *Platonic Lovers*; love-and-honour co-exists with an intense and explicit doubt of honour's worth. But only with the second way of escape was the reaction powerful enough. The first had to wait for *The Way of the World* and the third for *The Rehearsal*. But neither Congreve nor Buckingham and his friends could lay the ghosts of escapism. Libertinism and a belief in 'honour' are too precious to be easily foregone, and it was not the seventeenth century alone that knew them. Even Platonic Love, dormant in the Restoration, is a resurgent deity, animated often in the tales of disappointed old wives. So long as men fail to widen their angle of vision from sex to existence as a whole, so long do they need spectacles that change the focus of their sight,

[1] *The Dramatic Records of Sir Henry Herbert*, edited by Joseph Quincy Adams (Cornell Studies in English), 1917, p. 19.

so long do they turn to women as to wine, or think nobly of the soul, or impertinently proclaim:

> I could not love thee, dear, so much,
> Loved I not honour more.

Because of this narrowness of view in seventeenth-century dramatic poetry, so preoccupied with subjection to and escape from the flesh, the status of the drama is lowered: its lies are at times too apparent for esteem. Several times we are given acknowledgements of the fictitious basis of poetry. Thus in Davenant's *The Distresses* the heroine bewails the deceitfulness of true-love tales:

> *Ami.* O, how deceiving are those tragic tales:
> Those mourning histories of love, which, in
> The dreadful winter nights, our innocent maids
> Are us'd to read, whilst we are cozen'd of
> Our tears, weeping for joy, when loyal natures seem
> From hazard freed, and then for grief of their
> Distress. Yet now I see such characters
> Of honour ne'er had real being here.
>   *Orco.* 'Las! These are poets' snares to catch
> Young lovers in.   (IV. ii.)

In Heywood's *Loves Maistresse: Or, The Queens Masque* (1634) it is suggested that the noble tale of Troy and Helen was a poetic glorification of a village squabble over a light wench. And Davenant in *The Fair Favourite* (1638) looks back cynically to Sir Philip Sidney and finds his pastoral figures buried deep:

> *Thor.* . . . Where are the old Arcadian lovers?
> *Aler.* Why, in their graves, where they sleep quietly.
>   (I. i.)

Chapter 10

CATHOLIC AND PROTESTANT DRAMA

PART of the stock of common knowledge, imperceptively accumulated and rarely drawn upon, is that the Spanish and English dramas reached their zeniths in the same period. The defeat of the Armada set fire to the minds of Shakespeare's contemporaries, and his own plays were written in its afterglow: Lope de Vega was one of the survivors of that defeat, though an exceptional survivor, a poet, who wrote an epic poem during the voyage. But it is one thing to know of the time of the drama's triumph in Spain, and quite another to have read a play by Lope or by Calderón or by any one of the lesser dramatists who followed their fashion in play-writing. Of all the notable achievements in European literature, the Spanish drama of the sixteenth and seventeenth centuries is the least known to English readers.

There are good reasons for this neglect. According to his friend and biographer Montalbán, Lope de Vega wrote 1,800 full-length plays, 475 of which are extant and 361 in print.[1] Calderón wrote 121 plays, Tirso de Molina some three or four hundred, and others of his fellows maintained the tradition of fertility.[2] These figures are alone discouraging, but the English reader is further intimidated by the scarcity of good translations. As yet only seven of Lope's plays have appeared in English

[1] John Garrett Underhill, *Four Plays by Lope de Vega*, New York, 1936, pp. xix–xxi.
[2] *Ibid.*, p. xxiii.

versions, twenty-four of Calderón's, and one of Tirso's.[1] Moreover, the translations have rarely been good: Fitzgerald exercised his pen gracefully on Calderón, but imposed a Victorian discipline on the Spaniard's extravagance; Denis Florence MacCarthy, closely contemporary with Fitzgerald, was painstaking and often admirably ingenious in keeping to the forms of Calderón's verse, but his lines are too heavily intrinsicate for the dramas to stay alive; Henry Thomas's blank verse translation of Lope's *La estrella de Sevilla* (1935) makes Lope far too much like an Elizabethan of a paler hue; Harry Kemp's impetuous version of Tirso's *El burlador de Sevilla* (1923) casts a faint reflection of *The Yellow Book* on Velasquez' Spain. Rarely does one find a translation which suggests that these plays have possibilities on the modern stage: two notable exceptions are the version of Calderón's *La vida es sueño* by Frank Birch and J. B. Trend (1925) and that of Lope's *Fuente Ovejuna* by J. G. Underhill (1936). To read these, with some knowledge of the seventeenth-century Spanish theatre, is at once to realise that here was a drama vital, extravagant, taking its rise from the nature of the playhouse, speaking to and for the people assembled there, and capable of expressing both the recognised facts of common experience and the subtler perceptions native to a poet. In fact, here we recognise a face of things that we have known in the Elizabethan theatre.

The form of the Spanish theatre was not unlike the Elizabethan. The first public theatre to be built in Madrid dated from 1579: London had its 'Theatre' from 1576. In both the stage was a platform one, with a tiring-house behind it; the theatre was in early years open to the sky; spectators sat in the balconies or stood on the ground.

---

[1] Seventeenth-century plays drawing upon these writers, either directly or through a French channel, but not intended as versions of the Spanish originals, are not included in these numbers.

There were differences, of course: the Spanish playhouse used a back-cloth, it had a few benches on the ground near the stage, it did not develop the Elizabethan upper-stage until the theatres were roofed.[1] Clearly the theatres of the two nations were similar in general character, both socially and in the physical framework which they gave to their plays.

English and Spanish dramas at this time are known to be 'romantic'. Dramatists of both countries disregarded the practice of antiquity and the precepts of the Renaissance critics, and freely acknowledged their rebelliousness. Webster, in his preface to *The White Devil* (1612), says that popular taste must be served, and his public will not stomach the correctness that he himself admires; Lope de Vega in his *Arte nuevo de hacer comedias* (1609) shrugs over the rules and protests that they do not concern the playwright who serves the people. But it was not only in disregard of classical rules that the resemblance existed. In Lope and in Shakespeare, there is a prodigal capacity for characterisation that links the two men: the Spaniard lacks, of course, Shakespeare's knowledge of the more inward parts of human nature, but again and again he makes us think of Shakespeare in his younger years when impetuously he threw off a character, for the very delight in catching a hint of humanity in the tangles of circumstance. And in Calderón and in the Elizabethans generally, there is that intoxication with sound and image that makes it necessary for us to learn their language and their cast of mind before we should claim understanding of them: the Elizabethans carried on the tradition of Euphuism;

---

[1] J. B. Trend, "Calderón and the Spanish Religious Theatre of the Seventeenth Century", *Seventeenth Century Studies Presented to Sir Herbert Grierson*, 1938, p. 164. Cf. Wilhelm Creizenach, *The English Drama in the Age of Shakespeare*, 1916, p. 372, and the drawing of a seventeenth-century Madrid theatre in Lucien Dubech, *Histoire générale illustrée du théâtre*, 1931, ii. 196.

the Spanish playwrights knew Góngora, and his wild comparisons from the field of nature fill their plays with hyperbole. Men and words, in fact, were alike the interests of Spaniard and Elizabethan. The differences between Spain and England arose from a difference in outlook, dependent on the social and ideological contexts in which the playwrights lived.

This chapter is an attempt to describe the dominant types of seventeenth-century Spanish plays, and to suggest how, through the inevitable comparison, light is thrown on the social and religious complexion of Elizabethan drama. The writer cannot claim to be a specialist in Spanish drama and is largely dependent on translations for such knowledge as he has. But even a slight acquaintance with Spanish plays of the seventeenth century seems to strengthen one's grasp of English dramatic tendencies in that time.

It will be well to note first the type of Spanish drama which is furthest from the English stage and which is at the same time most characteristic of Spain. This is the *auto sacramental* which was performed regularly in the great cities on the feast of Corpus Christi. It was given, not in the ordinary theatre, but in the open air on a scaffolding (*tablado*) round which were grouped several cars (*carros*) which provided scenes for the action and dressing-room accommodation for the players. The *carros* arrived at the place of performance in a solemn procession, displaying actors and scenes and doubtless drawing the multitude to the public place where the *tablado* was set up. One is at once reminded of the English mystery-cycles, but the Spanish plays are not medieval but baroque, deriving from the Counter-Reformation and marked by a sureness of art that the Middle Ages rarely knew.[1] The

---

[1] Cf. J. B. Trend, *op. cit.*, pp. 169–71. Lucien Dubech, *op. cit.*, ii. 205, gives a drawing which reconstructs an *auto* performance.

writing of *autos* was an inevitable task of the successful dramatist, and Lope is said to have written four hundred of them in addition to his other plays,[1] but the form seems to have achieved its justification in the hands of Calderón. His *La divina Philothea* (1681), probably his last writing for the stage, illustrates the character of his *autos* and at the same time makes clear the type of mind which he brought to the writing of secular plays.

The central character, Philothea, represents the God-loving soul and also humanity before the Incarnation. She is attacked in her castle by the Demon, whose allies The World and Voluptuousness bring with them Paganism, Judaism, Heresy and Atheism. Voluptuousness corrupts The Understanding, and the Five Senses, faint through hunger, desert. But The Prince of Light comes and fights on the side of Philothea. He brings the sacramental bread, and so the Senses are won back. Faith converts The Understanding with the aid of Hearing (*i.e.* tradition as distinct from the written word). The Prince is wounded and disappears, but his presence remains in the sacramental bread, and the castle of Philothea is secure.

The theological ideas here treated come remarkably alive: not only is there a carefully worked out line of thought in the action, which is much fuller than this outline would suggest, but there is a vigour and sincerity in the writing. Any comparison with *The Castle of Perseverance*, which also has a castle as the allegorical symbol of man's shelter from his enemies, is soon abandoned, for Calderón in thought and expression is far distant from all the English morality writers and especially from the one who made such demands on the perseverance that he counselled.

The English reader cannot but recognise the skill of the Spanish dramatist, though he may be repelled by the

[1] J. G. Underhill, *op. cit.*, p. xx.

cast of mind it reflects. What we note especially from this *auto* is the extreme femininity of the conception of the soul: it is thought of as destined to be the bride of Christ, it is inevitably personified as female, and we feel how foreign this is, not merely to ourselves, but to the Elizabethans in their attitude towards human nature. A particularly sensitive reader may feel as disturbed by it as when medieval writers present the Virgin as a universal Jocasta.

When we turn to Calderón's plays for the theatre, we must always bear in mind that his outlook on life is basically that of the writer of *autos*. He may write light-heartedly often, and may sometimes touch on things, like the difficulties of writing poetry, which have no apparent relation to his religion, but in any seriously intended com-position we shall find the convinced Catholic speaking. In fact, most of his important plays are of a frankly religious character. Among them is *The Mighty Magician* (*El magico prodigioso*, c. 1627), which Shelley in part translated: it is a study in the conversion of a sceptic, a Spanish Faust. It reaches an impressive level in III. i, where the sleeping Justina feels the power of Lucifer's magic, but for those not entirely at one with Calderón in the matter of faith it has an oddly juvenile appearance, as if the playwright could not fully imagine the sceptic's state of mind. For modern readers a more striking though more puzzling play is *The Devotion of the Cross* (*La devocion de la cruz*, 1620). This has an odd story to tell:

Eusebio, not knowing their relationship, loves his sister Julia. They had been born, twins, beneath a cross on a mountain, and had at once been separated. Julia's father Curcio intends her for a convent, so Eusebio's love is surreptitious. Their brother Lisardo discovers it, chal-lenges Eusebio and is killed. So Julia goes to the convent, and Eusebio becomes a hunted man, turning bandit and general murderer. But always he bears a veneration for the cross, which is marked on his breast. He tries to carry off Julia from the convent, but he sees that she too has a cross on her breast: he draws back from the sensation of sacrilege and leaves her. She follows him, in male disguise, murdering lavishly to cover up her tracks. When she finds him in the mountains, his band is attacked by Curcio and his followers. Eusebio is wounded. Because of an earlier act of mercy, the aged priest Alberto has promised him that he will come to shrive him before his death: now he calls for Alberto, but dies just before he arrives. However, his soul is allowed to remain in his body after death, so that even at that late hour Alberto can shrive him. Julia, made aware of her guilt, is miraculously transported by the cross, back to her convent and away from a possible temporal punishment for her crimes.

The most fruitful comparison with English drama in this case is with Tourneur's *The Atheist's Tragedy*. There, too, an orthodox Christian view of things is postulated, and the righting of all things by the act of Heaven is the substance of the action. In both there is blood and lechery, in both the speeches can rise to a fine frenzy in the dramatist's awe at human evil. But Tourneur gives an impression of discontent with his own orthodox conclusion: the power of evil is so great as it is presented in his play that no mere smoothing out of wrongs in the fullness of time can dissipate the sense of fear and disbelief. Calderón can pile crime upon crime, look open-eyed on things that shake Tourneur, yet see the divine Philothea in Eusebio and contrive a special dispensation for him. His hero believes, honours his cross, and wins a post-mortem shrift. We see at once the isolation of Tourneur, the sceptic in spite of himself, the reliance of Calderón on an established ideology which can preserve himself and Eusebio against disaster. The frequent disorder of Elizabethan plays thus appears no surprising thing, an inevitable consequence of isolation. Whether it is better to err alone or in company, whether the solitary error may be nearer the truth than the congregate error, is something for each man to decide. But in general the English have tended towards isolation, the Spanish towards communion. Or, to put it in another way, Elizabethan drama is Renaissance, that of Calderón is baroque.

With these religious plays we may associate Calderón's essays in philosophic drama, of which the most famous is his *Life's a Dream* (*La vida es sueño, c.* 1631–5). This has considerable claims to be his finest work, as well as the one most attractive to readers of Shakespeare: it leaves the world of simple faith and its abstractions and penetrates beneath the superficies of things to question the very character of experience. From the time when Theseus sees the craft of poet and player as the illumination of shadows to the time when Prospero sees the most solid fabric of the universe melting before his gaze, Shakespeare was never far away from the conception that dominates *Life's a Dream*. In fact, it is likely that no poet has ever escaped the fascination of this idea: the reason why Calderón, and not Shakespeare or another Elizabethan, made a play out of it was that it demands a sound basis of belief in a supernatural scheme. If here we are dreaming, somewhere else we must sometime awake.

The scene of Calderón's play is Poland, where Basilio is king. He is wise in the stars and has learned from them that his son Sigismund will enslave his father and his people. So from birth Sigismund is kept a prisoner in the mountains, covered with chains and the skins of animals. When the succession to the throne is debated, Basilio reveals his son's existence and says he will bring him to the palace and test his use of power: if he proves vicious, he will be taken back to prison and told that the interlude was a dream. This happens. But the army revolts in his favour, not wishing for the foreign king that will succeed Basilio if Sigismund is disinherited. The prince believes that his second release from prison is also a dream, but comes ultimately to see that all human actions and triumphs are dreams that man must awaken from: he makes peace with his father, losing his brutal nature.

The most striking passages in the play are those spoken by Sigismund after his return to prison, when he is gradually approaching a view of life combining the practical and the mystical. In II. ii he sees that, though life may be a dream, it is consistent within itself, that in it good and bad have their appropriate effects:

> *Clotaldo.* . . . For the good we do, even in our dreams, does
> not miscarry. [*Exit.*
> *Sigismund.* That's true. Then let us curb this fierce vexation,
> This fury, this ambition, lest by chance
> We dream again. For we shall dream again.
> We are in a world so singular, that living
> Is only dreaming; and experience
> Teaches, that men who live, dream what they are
> Until they wake.[1]

When the soldiers come to make him their leader, he refuses to be hoaxed once more by life's illusions:

> No! No! I'll not again be fortune's plaything.
> I know that life is all a dream. Begone,
> You phantoms that assume to deadened senses
> A body and a voice, and yet in truth
> Have neither voice nor body!—I'll have no more,—
> I'll have no more of your feigned majesties,
> Of your fantastic pomps,—illusions
> That vanish at a breath,—like almond blossoms
> That wake too soon, imprudent, ill-advised,
> Only to scatter in the breeze and fall,

---

[1] This and other passages from *Life's a Dream* are taken from the translation by Frank Birch and J. B. Trend.

Their rosy petals withered and decayed
Shorn of their beauty, light, and ornament.
I know you. Yes! I know you. And I know
You come alike to every man that sleeps.
But I know better. There's no hoaxing me.
For I am disillusioned. I know well
That life's a dream.   (III. i.)

Then he comes to realise the necessity of encountering the dream as a dream, living it to the full but with a recognition that it is not 'real', that all we have and do and are is lent by God, that nothing, not even our life, is ours:

Why, life's so short,
We'll dream again, my soul, we'll dream again!—
Always remembering that we must wake
At the needlepoint of our enchantment. Yet
Knowing that we must wake, we shall the less
Be disenchanted; for we mock misfortune,
When we're prepared to meet it in advance.
And so, if we bear in mind that all our powers,
When most they seem assured, are only borrowed,
And must return again to him who lent them,
We may dare all things.   (III. i.)

Though, in the actual doing of one's will, it is better to assume the dream will last till that is done:

But soft! Suppose I wake before it's done?
Such things are better left unsaid, for fear
I fail of their performance.   (III. i.)

In any event, dream or reality, life demands the practice of virtue, which will make friends for us when we awake:

Lead on, then, fortune, to a throne!
Do not awaken me, if this be sleep.
If it be real, let me not sleep again.
But whether it's reality or dream,
To do what's right,—that's the important thing:

If it's reality,—because it's real;
If not,—why then, to win a friend or two
Against our waking.   (III. i.)

In III. iii he reminds himself that it is better not to become too firmly attached to the glories of a dream:

But stay your flight, my soul! These fickle honours
May vanish else. It would go hard with me
To have achieved so much, only so soon
To lose it. And the less I prize it now,
The less I'll feel the loss, when I awake.

He answers for himself the argument that in a transient dream one should cultivate transient things:

This is a dream! and so,
Let us be quick to dream of pleasure now,
Before it turn to pain.—
But soft! These reasons,
This argument of mine,—it rounds upon me.
I stand convicted. If this is a dream,
It is vainglory. Who would sacrifice,
For vain and human glory, glory that
Is real and divine? The good that's past,
Is it not always just a dream? Ask any
Of fortune's favourites. Not one but knows,
Beyond a doubt, that his remembered triumphs
Were so much dreaming.
If, then, I am doomed
To disillusion, if I know that pleasure
Is but a blaze of fire, which the wind
Will turn to dust and ashes, let me cling
To the divine, whose fame is everlasting;
Where joy is not a dream, nor majesty
A slumber.   (III. iii.)

Even if an Elizabethan could give us the same conclusions, there would not be this sureness of tone. For Calderón the underlying reality of the world is so firm that all its appearances may be deceiving without disaster coming on the man who is deceived. Bedrock remains, on which a man may sleep.

But, while we can see that this play is far from the Elizabethan model, it is much easier to accept than *The Devotion of the Cross*. Free from the sensuous personifications of the *auto* or the religious play, it puts a conception of life that is within the understanding of the foreign reader. The distinguishing mark of Calderón is that he can live equably within the scope of this conception.

Before leaving the religious plays of Spain, it is well to glance at one, not by Calderón, which puts forward a rather sterner view of life. This is *El burlador de Sevilla* (*c.* 1627) by Tirso de Molina. Here we see the religious play coming closer to tragedy than was possible in the orthodox mind of Calderón. Tirso's play is of historical interest, as the work in which Don Juan first makes an appearance in literature, but it has other qualities to attract us. Racily it tells of the escapades of its hero, leading up to the supper with the Statue. There is horror in the last scenes, where Juan enters the graveyard he cannot escape from, and these are nicely contrasted with the brisk seduction episodes which occupy the greater part of the play. Current morality is upheld, and Tirso's message is that faith without works is valueless.[1] Juan repents at last, begging time from the Statue that he may be shriven, but this is denied him. Then, however, Tirso reveals a new attitude. All through the play Juan's villainies have been so audacious, so hubristic, that our occasional pity for his victims is less strong than a reluctant sympathy

---

[1] Tirso showed the other side of the medal in his *El condenado por el desconfiado*, in which the lesson is that works will not avail for salvation without faith: a hermit, despairing of his salvation, is damned; a rogue and a blasphemer comes ultimately, through trust in God, to salvation. Dubech, *op. cit.*, ii. 214, suggests that *El burlador* was meant as a necessary counter to the rather Lutheran implications of this play.

with him. Now, forsaken of God, denied shrift in his hour of death, he remains Don Juan:

> I am myself again!
> I die: but before God and hell and earth,
> With my last breath I finish Don Juan!   (III. xxi.) [1]

So the tragic note can occasionally be struck in Spanish drama. When it comes, we experience a sense of shock, for it is opposed to the current of opinion and to the overt intention of the playwright. But in no congregation of men can the feeling quite be suppressed that somehow man is most himself, most admirable, when alone he confronts a mastering fate.

After the religious plays, one is inevitably led to consider the plays on the theme of 'honour'. This is the social religion of the hidalgo, rising from his consciousness of family rather than of class. It led to plays with violent endings, but these are rarely tragedies proper, because they are concerned more frequently with pointing a moral, the moral that at all costs honour is sacred, than with showing the individual at odds with fate. Thus plays like Calderón's *The Painter of Dishonour* (*El pintor de su deshonra*) are only technically tragedies: their effect on us is generally tiresome, because we have not the passionate Spanish concern with family relationships. Sometimes, however, the Spaniards do achieve the tragic note in the honour-play, when their sympathies become so vitally engaged by one of their characters that his misfortune becomes the focal point of attention. Then the social lesson is shifted to the background, and we see humanity suffering as in tragedy. This is the situation in Calderón's *The Mayor of Zalamea* (*El alcalde de Zalamea*):

A regiment under Don Lope comes to Zalamea. Don Álvaro, a captain, is billeted on Pedro Crespo, a rich

---

[1] Translated by Harry Kemp.

farmer: by a trick he sees Crespo's daughter Isabel, and the brawl which follows makes Don Lope order Álvaro to be billeted elsewhere. The regiment leaves at dawn, but Álvaro returns to Zalamea, carries off Isabel and rapes her. Crespo, immediately after hearing this, is told that he has been elected mayor. He goes to Álvaro, and offers him all his goods if he will marry Isabel. Álvaro, feeling secure under martial law, refuses contemptuously. Crespo arrests him and will not give him up to Lope. The King, Philip II, arrives: he admits that Crespo has a right to justice, though rebuking him for acting *ultra vires*. Crespo shows that Álvaro has been garrotted by his order, adding that Isabel has retired to a convent. The King makes him perpetual mayor of Zalamea.

Without doubt this is an odd play. The first two acts are delightful in their realistic picture of a country town, reminding us of passages in Heywood's *The English Traveller*. Lope, ever complaining of his bad leg, and Crespo, volatile and friendly, are finely drawn, and the scene in the second act where they sit at supper with Isabel and her young brother Juan, concluding with the serenaders' song coming to them through the window, is a delightful pastel. But in Act III all this goes to pieces. The rape shocks us because we could have no suspicion that the play was going to turn in this way. Álvaro, indeed, had not appeared particularly villainous. But perhaps we should remember Calderón's Spain: Isabel was a peasant-girl to the Captain, fair game, and Calderón may be suggesting that distress and violence are near the quiet surface of things, bringing a muddy dawn to the most placid and amusing of evenings.

The Mayor of Zalamea, indeed, is rather different from the majority of honour-plays in that the honour here belongs to a farmer, not a hidalgo. It suggests a consciousness of social problems between class and class that widens the scope of the play and enlists modern sympathy more readily. It is not so ambitious as *The Devotion of the Cross* or Calderón's other religious plays, but it comes close to us in a way that they cannot.

In Lope de Vega's *The Star of Seville* (*La estrella de Sevilla*) [1] we actually get a criticism of the 'honour' which compels obedience to a code even when such obedience runs contrary to what the intuition recognises for just. The play tells how the thirteenth-century King Sancho covets Estrella, known as the Star of Seville. He gets access to her brother Tabera's house, and is there found by Tabera, who pretends not to believe he is the King, though knowing it, and treats him so brusquely that the King plans his death. One Sancho Ortiz is recommended as a man for the task: he accepts it before learning whom he is to kill. Actually he is Tabera's friend and Estrella's betrothed. But he fulfils his promise. The King is at length shamed into acknowledging that the murder was of his planning, when he finds that Sancho will not reveal it and that Estrella forgives her lover. But, when Sancho is freed from official blame, he and Estrella feel that marriage is impossible for them and they go their several ways. One wonders if this ending is due to Lope's artistic integrity, as it may be, or if he was swayed by the realisation that his audience would not tolerate a marriage of a sister to her brother's murderer.

In III. vii Sancho, in agony over his deed, imagines himself in hell. His servant Clarindo humours him, and they talk of the 'honour' that they affect to find there. The implication is that Sancho's devotion to his word is not only wrong (in this instance) but altogether unfashionable, that the honour-code is not only tyrannous but a dead letter:

---

[1] This has been assigned to other writers than Lope, but its critical tone accords well with that of his best work. Cf. the translation by Henry Thomas (1935).

Clarindo. There stands the tyrant Honour,
Beset by all the countless doting fools
That suffer for his sake.
 Sancho. I'll join them too, then.
Honour, a fool, an honourable fool,
Would be your Honour's servant, one that yet
Has ne'er transgressed your laws.—"Friend, 'twas ill
  done.
True honour is to know not honour now.
What, look for me in yonder world, when I
Have now been dead these hundred thousand years!
Henceforth, my friend, let money be your quest.
Money is honour now. What did you do?"—
Fulfilled my promised word.—"A pretty jest!
Fulfil a promise? What simplicity!
To break a promise now is manliness."—
I rashly promised I would slay a man,
And slew him in my wrath, although I knew
He was my greatest friend.—"Oh, folly, folly!"
            (III. vii.)[1]

As in *The Mayor of Zalamea*, we have a social criticism implicit in the play. The King is tyrannous, it is he who ruins three lives: a code which supports such criminals is bad. Once again the scope of the play is widened, the moral lesson gives place to an awareness of destructive power which cannot quite destroy human goodness, and a tragic effect ensues.

But, whether we focus our attention on these exceptional dramas, or consider the general type of honour-play, we see at once a difference from the seventeenth-century English plays which use the theme.[2] Both before and after the Civil War, 'honour' was one of the dominant impulses in

---

[1] Translated by Henry Thomas.

[2] That there is an historical connection here between Spanish and English dramas is evident from Dryden's "I hate your *Spanish* Honour, ever since it spoil'd our *English* Plays" (quoted by Allardyce Nicoll, *Restoration Drama*, 1928, p. 179).

the tragic hero's mind. But, from its beginnings in Fletcher and Shirley to its apotheosis in Dryden, this 'honour' is an empty thing which the playwrights used as dramatic material without experiencing the emotion or the intellectual conception of the family that it takes rise from. Our own attitude to-day may be Lope's in *The Star of Seville*, but we can enter into the mind of Crespo in *The Mayor of Zalamea* and recognise as genuine the impulse which produced *The Painter of Dishonour*. The playwrights of the Restoration give us no such feeling of genuineness. 'Honour', as for most of them 'love', was an abstraction which pleased without being related to the business of living—something to have on the tongue, to make a fine sound with. Here, indeed, distant though many of the Spanish honour-plays are from us, we must recognise their superiority to the English in sincerity and understanding.

The honour-plays become for us most striking when the narrow theme widens to include an idea of social justice. There are, however, examples of social drama proper from the pen of Lope de Vega. In his *The King the Greatest Alcalde* (*El mejor alcalde el rey*) he treats of the tyranny of a noble, who carries off a peasant's bride and is made by the King to pay for his crime with death. The theme is much the same as in *The Mayor of Zalamea*, but now the stress is on the social injustice and not on the necessity of preserving family honour. This becomes apparent in many passages where the tyranny of rank is attacked. Thus in I. iv:

> What justice shall I find
> This side of heaven, he being a powerful man
> And richest in the kingdom? [1]

---

[1] Quotations from *The King the Greatest Alcalde* and *Fuente Ovejuna* are from the translations by J. G. Underhill.

And in III. ii:

>   To hands like these
> Must the long-suffering world confide its laws?
> The poor shall yield his honour to the rich
> And then acclaim him just! Only his will
> He holds for law, and he has power to kill!

In II. i the villainous hidalgo blames the structure of society for his guilt:

> Oh would to God you were my equal now!
> But you know well the baseness of your state
> Affronts my noble blood. . . .
> The world made these vile laws in ages gone,
> And I must yield to them, obedient.

The King is presented in a very idealised fashion, but Lope doubtless found that necessary and could, moreover, use him as a stick to beat the nobles, whose crimes came closer to the common people. Certainly this play puts directly a social doctrine that finds only fugitive expression in seventeenth-century English drama. Though Shakespeare's theatre was of the people, it dealt only incidentally and in a carefully indirect fashion with the crimes of the English ruling class.

Lope's masterpiece in this kind, the social play *par excellence* of the seventeenth century, was *Fuente Ovejuna* (*c.* 1610–20). Though it tactfully places its action in the past, the play is far too insistent on social justice to be regarded as a period-piece.

In 1476 there is war for the Spanish crown between Alonso of Portugal and Ferdinand of Aragon. The Commander Fernán Gómez de Guzmán makes the town Fuente Ovejuna his headquarters. There he preys on the peasants and their women. When he attacks Laurencia, a peasant-girl, her lover Frondoso drives him off. Later he interrupts their wedding, but she escapes from him and stirs the people to revolt. They attack and kill the

Commander and his men. This is reported to Ferdinand, who sends a judge to find out who is responsible. The peasants are severely tortured, but, when each in turn is asked for the names of the guilty ones, he will answer only: "Fuente Ovejuna." When Ferdinand hears of this and of the Commander's acts, he gives pardon freely.

What gives an air of uniqueness to this play is the fact that the centre of sympathy and interest is not an individual or even a nation, but a unified group belonging to one social class. Here, as in *The King the Greatest Alcalde*, Lope stands for the peasant against the hidalgo: again he idealises the King, but he has peopled his play with figures who win sympathy both as individuals and as representatives of their social group. Certainly his peasants are exceptional in the flesh and blood they wear so naturally, and Laurencia in particular is a triumph even for Lope, famous among Spaniards for his women.

This realism helps the effect when the time for revolt comes. Because Laurencia is human, and has won our sympathy, her cries of scorn against those who would endure oppression strike home to us as well as to her townsfolk:

> Here be it known
> Tyrants reign o'er us,
> We are ruled by traitors,
> Justice is there none. . . .

My face is bruised and bloody in this court of honest men. Some of you are fathers, some have daughters. Do your hearts sink within you, supine and cowardly crew? You are sheep, sheep! Oh, well-named, Village of Fuente Ovejuna, the Sheep Well! Sheep, sheep, sheep! Give me iron, for senseless stones can wield none, nor images, nor pillars—jasper though they be—nor dumb living things that lack the tiger's heart that follows him who steals its young, rending the hunter limb from limb upon the very margin of the raging sea, seeking the pity of the angry waves.

But you are rabbits, farmers,
Infidels in Spain,
Your wives strut before you
With the cock upon their train!
Tuck your knitting in your belts,
Strip off your manly swords,
For, God living, I swear
That your women dare
Pluck these fearsome despots,
Beard the traitors there!
No spinning for our girls;
Heave stones and do not blench.
Can you smile, men?
Will you fight?
Caps we'll set upon you,
The shelter of a skirt,
Be heirs, boys, to our ribbons,
The gift of the maidenry,
For now the Commander will hang Frondoso from a merlon
of the tower, without let or trial, as presently he will string
you all, you race of half-men, for the women will leave this
village, nor one remain behind! Today the age of Amazons
returns, we lift our arms and strike against this villainy, and the
crash of our blows shall amaze the world!   (III. i.)

Certainly if Spanish drama had given us nothing but this
play, we should still have to turn to it with serious attention. But, again we should remind ourselves, the very
individualism of English drama prevents the development
in it of a corresponding social animus. Elizabethans could
sink their egoisms in the emotion of patriotism, but that
was only while the Armada stuck in their minds. Later
they were always at odds with their community, satirising
town and court and puritans and every section of society
in turn. They never succeed in speaking for a social group
as something which they delight to belong to. Even
Dekker, with his surface-realism, writes of the London

citizens with a playful condescension. But Lope, for all his adventures in high society, knew the common people and wrote more passionately when they were his subject. He had the advantage that in Spain the Renaissance had not achieved the condition which made the individual always tend to stand alone, a condition which may produce greatness but frequently turns septic.

There remains the category of Spanish plays which is the largest in number and the one with the most extensive influence. This is the cloak-and-sword comedy (*comedia de capa y espada*), which began to affect the development of English drama as early as Fletcher. The general features of the type are well known: the characters are of noble birth, they are in love with each other or with their family honour, they go through dangerous adventures and come near disaster, and they move, at their best, with the *léger-de-pied* of a ballerina, and talk their way almost unperturbed through the mazes of the plot. Neither Calderón nor Lope nor any one of their contemporaries was serious when writing this form: it was a deliberate relaxation, in which their religious belief and their fugitive social perceptions found no place. Calderón has on occasion the lightest of touches, while Lope makes his mark with greater firmness: Calderón's *The Fairy Lady* (*La dama duende*), with its heroine who makes various apparently supernatural appearances to her lover, is as near to Indian-paper thinness as can be imagined, while Lope's *The Gardener's Dog* (*El perro del hortelano*), with its Countess who loves her secretary but cannot bring herself to marry him until the world wrongly thinks him of noble parentage, has a pleasant cynicism.[1] But these differences depend on the playwrights' individual tempers.

[1] This is not strictly a cloak-and-sword comedy, but in Spain the comic drama rarely moves far away from the spirit of this form, even when its manner is more realistic.

There are some Spanish plays which will not fit into the four categories already dealt with. Lope's *Castelvines y Monteses*, which is his version of the Romeo and Juliet story, and Calderón's *Luiz Pérez el Gallego* [1] are tragicomedies with affinities to the cloak-and-sword comedy but far more vigorous and distressful in their action. And there were farces (*entremeses*) performed between the acts of longer plays. But, in general, Spanish drama fits neatly into compartments. This gives us a key to its understanding, as well as clearly differentiating it from English drama. It is a commonplace that comedy and tragedy continually overlap in English, that an Englishman is rarely content to represent life from a single viewpoint throughout a whole play. This is due not merely to national temperament but to the lack of fixed contours in English thought. To take a particular viewpoint is to make an act of faith in that viewpoint, and faith has been an uncertain quantity in English dramatists since the Renaissance. The Spaniard had his fixed scheme of things: when he was writing seriously, he almost inevitably took up his orthodox position and sketched life as he saw it from the viewpoint thus imposed on him. If religion were his subject, there could be no blurring of the viewpoint, and the same was generally true if family honour were his subject. If, on the other hand, he chose to look at life without serious concern, his view of it was as of a graceful game, which hidalgos could play on weekdays when they had no immediate thought of shrift. Only rarely does this delicate division of thought break down, when the playwright is driven to question the validity of the system imposed on him. Most clearly we have seen this happening when the writers turned from honour to social justice, and it is interesting, whether relevant or not, that in the Spain of

[1] The title of this play was changed by Fitzgerald to *Gil Perez, the Gallician*.

this century the conflict has been between an autocratic system, ecclesiastical and civil, and a rising consciousness of social wrong. In any event, *Fuente Ovejuna* was revived in Spain, after long neglect, during the present century.[1]

But, because of the general maintenance of the three-fold division of dramatic thought—religion, honour, and cloak-and-sword—the tragic spirit hardly existed. That comes when the world oppresses through its very lack of pattern, when the resolution of the individual alone withstands the erratic lightning: tragedy or a helter-skelter into the abyss can then equally be the result, according to the degree of the resolution. The Elizabethans and Jacobeans knew both, but Spain's ark of covenant with its god survived the Armada.

[1] J. G. Underhill, *op. cit.*, p. 278.

INDEX

227

INDEX

INDEX

INDEX

INDEX

DAVID GLENN HUNT
MEMORIAL LIBRARY
GALVESTON COLLEGE

DAVID GLENN HUNT
MEMORIAL LIBRARY
GALVESTON COLLEGE